# SUNDAY'S HEROES

## NFL LEGENDS TALK
## ABOUT THE TIMES OF THEIR LIVES

RICHARD WHITTINGHAM

## TRIUMPH
BOOKS
CHICAGO

Library of Congress Cataloging-in-Publication Data

Whittingham, Richard, date–

      Sunday's heroes : NFL legends talk about the times of their lives / Richard Whittingham.

        p. cm.

      Includes bibliography, index.

      ISBN 1-57243-517-8 (hc)

       1. Football—United States—Humor. 2. Football players—United States—Anecdotes. 3. National Football League.  I. Title.

GV950.5.W45 2003

796.332'64—dc21

                                        2003042671

"Blocking backs and interference

Fifty thousand wild adherents

Tackle thrusts and headlong clashes

Two-yard bucks and dizzy dashes

Head and shoulder, heart and soul

'Till you fall across the goal.

Football."

**—GRANTLAND RICE**

# Contents

# FOREWORD

I am tremendously proud to have had the opportunity to play and coach in the National Football League, and I say that in all honesty.

I grew up in Aliquippa, Pennsylvania, and naturally followed the Philadelphia Eagles and the Pittsburgh Steelers, at least for the most part. When I got to the NFL I had the experience of playing with three great teams: the Bears, the Eagles, and the Cowboys. Later I coached in Dallas, Chicago, and New Orleans.

When we played the game, we played with intensity and spirit. Over the years, professional football has been filled with wonderful athletes, fierce competitors, and unique individuals—great human beings on and off the field. The game has become huge, reaching tens of millions of people. It was and is our game, and we are proud of it.

I don't think there are a lot of reasons to be changing everything every year—we must be careful not to take what is good about the product and change it. NFL football has been played for a long time—80-some years—and will be played for at least 80 more. We should not spend our time worrying about making the game shorter or speeding it up or that kind of crap. If it's a good game, it's a good game. Think of all the great individual games we've been fortunate to watch; think of all the great performances, the great plays, the great team efforts. *That's* NFL football. We have to be careful not to lose sight of the game itself and the glory connected with it.

—**Mike Ditka**

# AUTHOR'S PREFACE

**W**hile doing research for a book some years ago, I sat down to lunch in Canton, Ohio, with Pete Elliott, then the director of the Pro Football Hall of Fame, and Joe Horrigan, the curator of that organization's library and archives. Of course, we talked about football. Actually, we began telling stories about the players, coaches, and owners we'd encountered; some of the stories were funny, others insightful, still others eyebrow-raising. One story led to another; it was the kind of thing that goes on routinely at NFL team reunions and in sports bars throughout the country.

Sometime later it occurred to me that, because I was fortunate enough to have access to such stories—through interviews I conducted for the books I was doing, or merely through the times spent over lunch tables or at those bars where football is the conversation of choice—it might be a good idea to record and pre-serve them for posterity. It would be a terrible shame if somehow they got lost over time, because these are the stories about the human side of professional football. They are tales told by or about the great athletes who played the game; by the coaches they feared, or respected, or both; and by the owners they hated or loved. They are about the characters involved with the game and, believe me, there have been an abundance of characters over the years. These anecdotes and stories are about the heroes and the clowns, about the stars and the bench sitters.

Here we have George Halas revealing the story of why his enforcer, George Trafton, once had to run for his life after a game. Here Johnny Blood McNally remembers the infamous Mother Pierre's whorehouse, and Pete Gent recalls forever surprising his coach, Tom Landry. We read of Doug Williams fielding the question: "How long have you been a black quarterback?" Here Roger Staubach responds to the image he was saddled with, and George Preston Marshall defines the monumen-tal importance of his beloved Redskins marching band.

There are presidential messages from LBJ, Nixon, and Reagan, as well as Gerald Ford, who actually played against the pros (the Chicago Bears in the 1935 College All-Star Game). Here Red Grange tells of his fabled barnstorming tour of 1925, during which he had a White House audience with President Calvin Coolidge.

Dick Butkus remembers pain and colliding with Jim Brown. Frank Gifford recalls strange happenings in New York City. Many reminisce about the immortal

Vince Lombardi. "Dandy" Don Meredith offers some characteristically unique insights. Lone Star Dietz proves coaching is not restricted to orthodox methods.

And there's Duane Thomas with his special take on the Super Bowl; the idiosyncrasies of Joe Don Looney; the Hawaiian penal colony hangman who aspired to a career in the NFL. . . . Jungle Jamey . . . Bubbles Cash . . . Two-Bits Homan . . . and Abe Cohen and the sneakers that saved the day.

Sunday's heroes are indeed a unique and entertaining lot.

# INTRODUCTION

**M**y entire adult life I've been associated with professional football. I came to the NFL back in 1952 when I was 22 years old and just out of the University of Arkansas. The Lions drafted me that year, and it was a big change from college football. I'd played in that year's College All-Star Game and in the preseason with the Lions, but then I broke my arm and was out for the rest of the year.

Detroit had quite a team then, some great players like Bobby Layne and Doak Walker and Leon Hart; they were a fascinating group of characters, a very tightly knit group. Led by Layne, they traveled and lived with a lot of flash: you followed him, you stayed up late and played hard, both on and off the field.

One of the things I remember about those days is that they gave me a kicking shoe, a square-toed, specially made shoe. Back then pro teams didn't furnish you with a pair of shoes. You brought along the ones you'd used in college. But I got a kicking shoe.

At the same time, I was not a kicking specialist; they didn't exist in those days. You played, and sometimes you played 60 minutes. I was an end on offense and defense besides being the kicker. You had to play; the roster was limited to 33 players in the early fifties, so you had to do more than one thing. No team could afford to carry a specialist or a third quarterback. I was on all the special teams, too: kick returns, punt returns, covering punts. And we all worked in the off-season. We weren't expected to stay in playing shape all year round like the players are today, and we weren't paid enough to do that. Everyone had a side job; I taught school back in my hometown, Lake City, Florida, in the off-season.

After sitting out my rookie year, I was traded to the Cardinals, who were playing in Chicago then. Charlie Trippi was still there, but the Dream Backfield (which also included Paul Christman, Elmer Angsman, and Pat Harder) was long gone, the team was in a state of major decline, and Trippi was at the end of his career. Going from the Lions, who won the NFL title in 1952 (and would win it again in 1953) to the Cardinals, who were near the bottom of their conference, was a real awakening. The Lions had an esprit de corps, a real sense of pride; they thought and acted like winners. In Chicago, the equipment was poor and the facilities were bad; Comiskey Park was no vacation spot.

My first practice, I remember well. We were working out at the University of Chicago because the White Sox were still playing at Comiskey, and the stands were covered with tar paper and some funny-looking smokestacks were coming out of them. I said to Johnny Olszewski, our fullback, "What the heck is that? It looks so depressing." He said under there's where they invented the atom bomb.

Our captain was Jack Jennings, a character out of the old mold; he was a tackle out of Ohio State, and he had an off-season job with the makers of Jim Beam whiskey, a job he maintained through the season as well. I remember one day he missed most of practice and got there just about the time we were finishing up with wind sprints. He had slept in his hat, and the ring from it was still around his head; the cloves he was chewing were literally falling out of his mouth. He said he had had a tough night. Another time when we were out together, he'd had much too much of the Jim Beam and called his wife and told her to trace the call and come pick him up.

After several years with the Cardinals, I was thinking about getting out of the game. It was a sad situation—we had only one winning year when I was there (1956)—and it was a miserable operation in Chicago. Just after the 1957 season, we got a new coach; Pop Ivy replaced Ray Richards. I went to him and asked where I stood, where I fit in. Pop told me, "You're a key part of the team, Pat, a key part of the operation. Yes! We want you back."

A week or so later I was over at the post office down where I lived in Lake City, Florida, and picked up the afternoon paper and saw that I'd been traded to the Giants.

The Giants turned out to be a wonderful experience. We had some great teams, some great players: Frank Gifford, Charlie Conerly, Kyle Rote, Alex Webster, Sam Huff, Rosey Grier, Jim Katcavage, Andy Robustelli, Dick Modzelewski, Jim Patton. They were a special cast of characters, and we were the kings of New York.

The most outlandish was Cliff Livingston, a linebacker from UCLA; he came back each year as a different guy. He changed personalities. One year he came back and told us he was Robin Hood—bow and arrow and all—and that his plan was to rob from the rich and give to the poor. I was rooming with him that year, and one night when the season was almost over I woke up and saw him standing there with the bow drawn back and the arrow aimed at me. I said, "What the hell are you doing? Are you crazy?" He just looked back and said, "What are you doing here? Who are you?" He didn't seem to know, although we'd been roommates for weeks. At any rate, he didn't shoot me. Another year he came to training camp and told us he was a race car driver, another he was the world's greatest lover. That year, after playing a preseason game against the Cowboys, he showed up at the Dallas airport to get on the team plane wearing only leopard-skin bikini shorts. He walked all the way through the airport like that, barefoot, and got on the plane. Another time, we had an exhibition game in Hershey, Pennsylvania. After the game, he wasn't on the team airplane, which was flying out of Harrisburg. When the plane moved out to the runway, a taxicab was chasing it across the airfield. Cliff was in it. They stopped the plane and opened the door and let down the steps and he clambered on board, and then he borrowed some money to pay off the cab driver.

For a couple of years there we had both Vince Lombardi and Tom Landry as our assistant coaches, Vince for the offense and Tom for the defense. They were magnificent, and they would listen to you, to the players. If you came up with an idea, say a pass pattern you thought could work, you'd say, "Hey, Vinny [we called him Vinny, but the Packers never did], I think this might work." He'd listen and if it made sense he'd run it and sometimes he'd say, "Hey, I think we got something here," and maybe put it into the game plan.

My personal highlight, of course, was the field goal in the snow against the Browns in 1958 that clinched a tie for us in the NFC East. But there were others, too. I remember for a while there in 1959 our offense wasn't doing so well but our defense was great. It seems the only way we were scoring was on field goals; in fact in two back-to-back games we scored just nine points each. That's what prompted NFL commissioner Pete Rozelle, when he was told the following week that the Giants beat the Cardinals 30–20, to say, "What happened? Did Summerall kick 10 field goals?"

After the 1961 season, I retired. But I had already begun my second career within the NFL. It came about earlier, after we had played a preseason game against the Packers in Newark. We were training at that time in Bear Mountain, New York, up near West Point. The game was on a Friday night, and we did not have to be back in camp until Monday night. So a bunch of us got together and went into Manhattan for the weekend. I shared a room with Charlie Conerly. The phone rang— I was lying on the bed and he was in the shower—and it was this gentleman asking for Charlie. I told him he was in the shower, and he said to remind Charlie that he was supposed to come to CBS that afternoon at 4:00 to read for this radio show.

I was maybe an inch away from hanging up the telephone when the guy said, "Hey, wait a minute. What are you doing this afternoon?"

I said, "I don't know, maybe going to a movie, maybe going out for a beer. Why?"

"Why don't you come along and take the audition, too?" he said.

I said, "Why not?" As it turned out, there were four of us who went over to CBS that day. And I ended up getting the job.

And that's been a great experience as well. There are a lot of memories from the more than 40 years I've been doing NFL broadcasts. And the greatest of them has been the contact with the players—the colorful ones, the crazies, the ones with the short fuses, the ones who didn't want to talk, and the ones you could not get to stop talking.

I especially remember the first Super Bowl, although it wasn't called that the first year. It was January 1967, out at the Coliseum in Los Angeles, and the Packers were playing the Kansas City Chiefs. It wasn't a sellout crowd by any means—a lot of empty seats. The game was covered by two networks. Four announcers handled it for CBS: myself, Frank Gifford, Jack Whitaker, and Ray Scott; and two covered it for NBC: Curt Gowdy and Paul Christman. There was none of the hype that we now associate with the game; in fact, nobody really wanted to play the game. Nobody thought Kansas City had a chance against Lombardi's Packers. I remember being down on the sideline behind the Packers' bench and NBC missed the second-half kickoff because they hadn't wrapped up their interview with Bob Hope, who happened to be at the game. So they sent word down to me—being the broadcaster on the sideline—asking me to ask Lombardi if he'd mind kicking off again. I said, "What? You want me to ask Vince Lombardi if *he* would kick off again for you guys? You've got to be kidding. If not, you've sure got the wrong guy."

Super Bowl X was another oddity, for me at least. That was in 1976, and the Steelers were playing the Cowboys. The game was at the Orange Bowl in Miami. I was doing the game with Tom Brookshier, but he had a cold, and halfway through the first quarter he began losing his voice. There was nobody else there, so I ended up doing practically the whole game by myself. He squawked out a word or two once in a while, but that was about it; every time I turned around in the booth, someone was spraying his throat.

I did 26 Super Bowls over the years on radio and television, as an analyst in five or six and doing the play-by-play in the rest. And I haven't any idea how many pre-, post- and regular-season games I did.

All I can say is, it's been a great run.

—PAT SUMMERALL

# SUNDAY'S HEROES

Game action, 1933: the Boston Redskins take on the Portsmouth Spartans at Fenway Park. The high-flying ball carrier for Portsmouth is Ace Gutowsky; the helmetless Spartan is Roy "Father" Lumpkin (No. 57). Portsmouth won that day, 13–0. The next year the Spartans would move to Detroit and change their name to the Lions; four years later the Redskins would move to Washington.

# 1

## Soft Helmets, Hard Heads

"Football is a wonderful way to get rid of aggressiveness without going to jail for it."

**W**hen the National Football League was founded in 1920, the Bears were in Decatur, Illinois (and known as the Staleys), and the Cardinals were in Chicago—they were the only franchises that remain in the league today. Other charter-member teams among the 14 teams that first year of the NFL were from Muncie, Indiana; Canton, Ohio; Rock Island, Illinois; Rochester, New York; and Hammond, Indiana (and the best among them were the undefeated Akron Pros). The Green Bay Packers came along the following year, the New York Giants in 1925, but it was a long evolutionary process for the NFL to become the institution as we know it today.

When the league got underway in the twenties, the players were much smaller: linemen weighed between 180 and 220 pounds, with an occasional behemoth reaching 240, and they ranged in height from 5'10" to 6'2". Some backs were no more than 5'6" and 150 pounds. There were ordinarily 18 to 22 players on a roster, and starters played 60 minutes. Their helmets were made of soft leather, and some players declined to wear one. There were no face guards, and it was a rare player who retired from the game with all his original teeth and a nose that didn't bend or bob one unorthodox way or another.

Until 1925, a team was lucky if five thousand people showed up at a game, much less paid to get into it. Starting players' salaries averaged between $100 and $200 a game—a true star might get as much as $400—paid in cash, usually right after each game. This was the same era in which a major college football game might draw as many as seventy thousand fans.

The appearance in 1925 of Red Grange, college football's most illustrious hero, launched the NFL in the direction of a true big-league sport. Joining the Bears and accompanying them on a barnstorming tour of the United States after the '25 regular season, the "Galloping Ghost" inscribed the game of professional football on the American sporting scene. More than seventy-two thousand filled the Polo Grounds to watch Grange and the Bears play the New York Giants that winter; an even larger crowd flooded the Los Angeles Coliseum a few months later when the barnstorming tour took Grange and the Bears to California to face a made-for-the-occasion West Coast All-Star team.

In those early days, the game of professional football was different in certain respects from how it is played today. Passing was a rarity, games took about two hours from start to finish, and records and statistics were only loosely kept. But the sport was as intense and brutal, the players as rugged and talented, the games as hard-fought and as exciting as they are today.

And it certainly was just as entertaining, on the field and off the field.

The appearance in 1925 of Red Grange, college football's most illustrious hero, launched the NFL in the direction of a true big-league sport.

## ALONG COMES THE MENACE . . .

In 1923, legendary college football coach Amos Alonzo Stagg addressed the issue of professional football and the infant National Football League in a letter "To all friends of college football," which he released to the Associated Press:

> **For years the colleges have been waging a bitter warfare against the insidious forces of the gambling public and alumni and against overzealous and shortsighted friends inside and out, and also not infrequently against crooked coaches and managers who have been anxious to win at any cost, and victory has not been completely won. And now along comes another serious menace, possibly greater than all others, viz., Sunday professional football.**
>
> **Under the guise of fair play but countenancing rank dishonesty in playing men under assumed names, scores of professional teams have sprung up within the last two or three years, most of them on a salary basis of some kind. . . .**
>
> **Cases of the debauching of high school boys not infrequently have come to notice. Also recently one of the well-known Sunday professional football teams on which several men are said to be regularly playing under assumed names employed a well-known [Big Ten] conference official who officiated under an assumed name. . . .**
>
> **To cooperate with Sunday professional football games is to cooperate with forces which are destructive of the finest elements of interscholastic and intercollegiate football and to add to the heavy burden of the schools and colleges in preserving it in its ennobling worth. . . .**

## LET OLD JIM RUN

The power of Jim Thorpe was legendary. And no one told a tale of that power better than Knute Rockne, the fabled Notre Dame coach who also played for the pros in the early days of the game.

Rockne was a defensive end for the Massillon Tigers, and Thorpe was in the backfield for the Canton Bulldogs when they first encountered each other on a football field. On his first carry, Thorpe was met by Rockne at the line of scrimmage and brought down with a good tackle. When they got up, Thorpe said, "Rock, you shouldn't do that." He nodded over to the spectators on the sideline, "Those folks, they come to see Old Jim run. Be a good boy and let Old Jim run."

A few plays later, Rockne broke through and tackled Thorpe for a loss of a couple of yards. "Rock, you're not letting Old Jim run. Those folks aren't going to be happy. You've got to let Old Jim run."

"Those folks, they come to see Old Jim run. Be a good boy and let Old Jim run."

—JIM THORPE

**Artist Dave Boss captures the power of the legendary Jim Thorpe.**

Like hell, Rockne thought, more than a little pleased with the way he was handling the game's most famous player while at the same time a little dismayed at how overrated the mighty Native American was, or so it seemed to him.

On the next play, Rockne broke through again and lowered his head to take on Thorpe. This time Thorpe lowered his head and shoulder, too, and met Rockne full blast. The impact was shattering, and Rockne went down in a heap, alone and stunned. Through the fog that enshrouded his brain, the Rock heard the roar of the crowd. When he finally staggered to his feet, he saw Thorpe in the end zone, some 50 yards downfield, holding the ball triumphantly above his head. Then Thorpe trotted back upfield and patted the dazed Rockne on the shoulder pads. "That's the way, Rock," he said. "You let Old Jim run."

### RUNNING FOR HIS LIFE

George Trafton, the Hall of Fame center who played for the Chicago Bears in the twenties and early thirties, was well known for his ferocity on the field. In a game in 1920, when the Bears were known as the Decatur Staleys, against the Rock Island Independents he sent several players to the sideline with assorted injuries. The crowd, already angry, became even more enraged when Rock Island fullback Fred Chicken joined the casualty list after encountering Trafton.

"I tackled him right on the sideline," Trafton said. "There was a fence close to the field, and after I hit Chicken he spun up against [it] and broke his leg. After that the fans were really on me"—an understatement to say the least. At the end of the game, they chased Trafton out of the stadium and down the street under a shower of rocks, empty bottles, and anything else they could find. Dutch Sternaman, halfback (and halfowner) of the Staleys, tried to pick him up in a taxicab Sternaman had commandeered, but the pursuers were too close. Trafton eventually managed to escape with the help of a passing motorist who was evidently not an Independents fan.

The next time the Staleys/Bears appeared in Rock Island, the game was again especially physical, and the crowd grew almost as angry as they had at the previous meeting. When the game ended and coach and half owner George Halas was handed $7,000 in cash, the visiting team's share of the gate receipts, he gave the

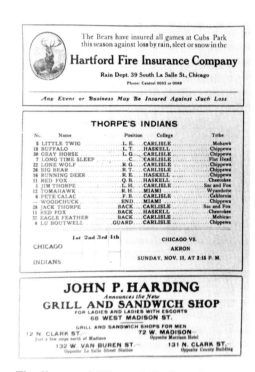

The lineup of "Thorpe's Indians," actually the Oorang Indians of Marion, Ohio, in 1923. Despite the great Thorpe at halfback, his Indians were 1–10–0 that year, a lowly 18th place in the 20-team NFL of 1923.

money to Trafton for safekeeping. As Halas later told the story: "I knew that if trouble came, I'd be running only for the $7,000. Trafton would be running for his life."

### PURITY OF PURPOSE

The Packers issued this policy statement of purity in 1921 when they formally joined the National Football League:

### POLICY OF THE GREEN BAY FOOTBALL CORPORATION

The policy of the GREEN BAY FOOTBALL CORPORATION is to promise clean, healthful sport; to maintain for the City of Green Bay a football team that will be a leader in this great American out-door [sic] sport. The team is composed of former College stars and will have the leading football teams of the country as opponents. Our City will gain added publicity in supporting games that will attract nation-wide [sic] attention and be recognized as a promoter of clean sports and recreation. Financial gain derived from the season's playing is donated to the American Legion.

Action from the Boston Braves' (later the Boston Redskins and still later the Washington Redskins) first game, an exhibition against the semipro Quincy Trojans in 1932. At top, Tony Plansky carries for an 18-yard touchdown. Bottom, Jim Musick gathers in a lateral on his way to the Braves' second touchdown of the day. Boston won easily that afternoon, and went on to compile a 4–4–2 regular-season record, fourth best in the eight-team NFL of 1932.

Center George Trafton was one of the most fearsome linemen of the twenties. Out of Notre Dame, he joined the Decatur Staleys in the NFL charter year of 1920 and stayed with the team after it became the Chicago Bears through the 1932 season. The first center to use the one-handed snap, he was also one of the best defensive linemen in the game. Trafton was inducted into the Pro Football Hall of Fame in 1964.

## MARSHALL'S CODE OF CONDUCT

In the thirties, Washington Redskins owner George Preston Marshall, as fastidious as he was stubborn, published a code of conduct for his players and distributed it:

> **You will be expected to conduct yourselves in such manner as to always be a credit to the game and your club.**
>
> **Violation of publicly accepted and traditional training rules for athletes—rowdiness, boisterousness, and ungentlemanly conduct of any and every sort—will not be tolerated.**
>
> **In hotel lobbies, dining rooms and restaurants, and at all public functions where the team appears as a unit, shirts, ties, and coats are to be worn unless otherwise instructed.**
>
> **Nightclubs, bars, cocktail lounges, and gambling spots are definitely out of bounds.**

## HEALEY AND HALAS

In Myron Cope's *The Game That Was,* Hall of Fame tackle Ed Healey remembered a game between the Rock Island Independents and George Halas' Chicago Bears:

> **[Speaking to one of the game's referees] "Now, Roy, I understand to start with that you're on the payroll of the Bears. I know that your eyesight must be failing you, because this man Halas is holding me on occasion and it is completely destroying all the things that I'm designed to do in that line." I said, "Roy, I'll tell you what I'm gonna do. In the event that Halas holds me again, I am going to commit mayhem. As a matter of fact, I am going to attempt to take his block right off those shoulders of his."**
>
> **Now bear in mind, please, that we had a squad of about 15 or 16 men. Neither Duke Slater, our right tackle, nor I had a substitute on the bench. So I said, "Roy, you can't put me out of the game, because we don't have another tackle. And I can't really afford to be put out of this ballgame because of your failure to call Halas' holding. I have notified him, and I am about to commit mayhem."**
>
> **Well, the condition of the field was muddy and slippery—a very unsafe field. Halas pulled his little trick once more, and I come across with a right, because his head was going to my right. Fortunately for him, he slipped somehow—or maybe I slipped—and my fist went whizzing right past that head of his, right into the terra firma, which was soft and mucky. My fist was buried. When I pulled it out, it was with an effort like a suction pump. But I'm telling you, I felt very, very happy that I had not**

"In the event that Halas holds me again, I am going to commit mayhem. As a matter of fact, I am going to attempt to take his block right off those shoulders of his."

—HALL OF FAME TACKLE
ED HEALEY

connected. I'm just telling you that, had I connected, I might have dismantled Halas. So I was happy that I hadn't, because this was on a Sunday and on the following Tuesday, I believe it was, I was told to report to the Bears. George Halas had bought me for a hundred dollars.

## DUTCH CLARK REMEMBERS

Earl "Dutch" Clark, a member of the Pro Football Hall of Fame who led the NFL in scoring three times during his seven-year career with Portsmouth and later Detroit in the thirties, remembered his early days in the pros in *The Game That Was*:

In 1931, I signed with Portsmouth for $140 a game. That was good money. A lot of players made $95 or $100, and even then you didn't get all your pay.

They said the first game was a practice game, so we would get only $35. But the first game happened to be against Brooklyn, a league team, actually the league opener, yet they gave us only $35. It was in the contract—"first game." What could you do?

Portsmouth was a town that was crazy about football. There were maybe thirty-five, forty thousand people in the town. The Selby shoe factory was there, but

Action from a Green Bay Packers–Chicago Bears game of 1936. Vaulting over the pile is Packers tackle Ade Schwammel; identifiable Bears are Bronko Nagurski (No. 3), and Ookie Miller (No. 76). The Pack was 10–1–1, edging out the 9–3–0 Bears in the NFL West, then drubbing the Boston Redskins 21–6 for the league title.

The ever-unpredictable and always colorful Shipwreck Kelly (left) with fellow Brooklyn Dodger Benny Friedman in 1933. Kelly, a fleet halfback and top pass receiver, played a year with the New York Giants, then three with Brooklyn, a franchise he bought in partnership with former Army great Red Cagle in 1933. Friedman, a tailback and the best passer of his time, had a fine NFL career from 1926 through 1934, most notably with the Giants and the Dodgers.

the people weren't working. So at practice, when we were going to scrimmage, we would have maybe five thousand people out watching us. If we didn't scrimmage, they'd scream and holler. Then we'd get up to the day of the game, and we wouldn't have two thousand people there. They were nice people in Portsmouth, but they didn't have the money.

In Portsmouth the ballplayers slept in rooming houses scattered around town. You'd pay maybe $1.50 or $2.00 a week for a room, and you could get the biggest meal in town for six bits, probably.

### HALL OF FAME OVERSIGHT?

Giants' owner Wellington Mara had only the fondest of memories for quarterback Benny Friedman, whose services the Giants enjoyed for three years (1929–31):

"Automatic Jack" Manders kicks a last-minute, game-winning (10–9) field goal for the Chicago Bears against the New York Giants at the Polo Grounds to preserve a perfect 13–0 regular season in 1934. Helmets, needless to say, were not mandatory then: witness Manders, his holder Carl Brumbaugh, and end Bill Hewitt (blocking No. 36). Shortly thereafter the Giants ruined that year for the Bears by defeating them in the NFL title game, 30–13.

Benny Friedman was our first really big star. He had been with Cleveland [the Bulldogs] and Detroit [the Wolverines] but both those teams had folded. In fact, my father had bought out the remnants of the Detroit team and brought Friedman in here. Benny Friedman made a great contribution to pro football in New York, off the field as well as on it. Several times a week he would go around to high school assemblies in the mornings and give tickets away to promote the game. He was, of course, a fine player, and a durable one. I don't think he ever missed a game because of an injury. Benny Friedman truly deserves to be in the [Pro Football] Hall of Fame. He was one of the real pioneers of the game . . . [he] was one of a kind and never got the proper recognition.

### ROONEY ON THORPE

Art Rooney, beloved owner of the Pittsburgh franchise in the NFL (first the Pirates then the Steelers) played semipro football in Pittsburgh in the early twenties. He recalled this encounter:

> I remember we played the Canton Bulldogs and Jim Thorpe in Pittsburgh once. I tried a field goal but it was blocked. Thorpe picked it up and ran for a touchdown, and as I recall, they beat us, 6–0. Oh, I played against Thorpe a number of times. He was certainly fast, but Thorpe was pretty much at the end of his rope then. Anyhow, the game in those days was just shoving and pushing, compared to what it is now.

Ed Healey, from Dartmouth, joined the Rock Island, Illinois, Independents in the NFL's first year, 1920. Two years later his contract was bought by George Halas, co-owner of the Chicago Bears, for $100 in one of the first player deals ever made in the new league. A great tackle on both offense and defense, Healey stayed with the Bears through 1927 and was elected to the Pro Football Hall of Fame in 1964.

### BELOIT BEATS THE PACKERS

In 1919, two years before the Green Bay Packers joined the NFL, they suffered a defeat at the hands of a team ignobly named the Beloit Fairies—although the news story about the game failed to report the team's nickname. Here's that story, excerpted from *The Packers* by Steve Cameron:

> BELOIT, Wis., November 24—The Green Bay Packers met defeat at the hands of the Beloit Professionals at Morse Park on Sunday by the score of 6 to 0 before a good-sized crowd of spectators.

Earl "Dutch" Clark, one of the greatest tail-backs of the early game, came out of tiny Colorado College and joined the Portsmouth Spartans in 1931. A triple-threat back, he stayed with them through the name change to the Detroit Lions, earning All-Pro honors in six of his seven years in the NFL. He led the league in scoring in 1932, 1935, and 1936. Clark entered the Pro Football Hall of Fame in 1963.

Capt. [Earl "Curly"] Lambeau's team was robbed of victory by referee Zabel of Beloit. This official penalized Green Bay three times after touchdowns, refusing to allow the scores. The Packers were twice on the verge of leaving the field but decided to play it out.

Every time the Packers had the ball, the crowd would sweep out on the playing field, leaving practically no room for the forward pass offensive and, of course, in this way, putting a big check on the Packers' ground gaining machine.

Just before the close of the game, McLean got away for a long run, headed goalward, close to the sidelines, when a Beloit spectator gave him a foot and the Green Bay quarterback fell to the ground.

## WHY THE BURLESQUE GIRLS LOVED ART ROONEY

Abby Mendelson, in his book *The Pittsburgh Steelers: The Official Team History*, offered this vignette about the fabled owner of the Pittsburgh Steelers:

In the old days, when every man wore a tie and the Edison [a Pittsburgh hotel] was less raffish, the Casino was a downtown burlesque house. On an evening, Art Rooney would play cards at the Edison, sometimes until one in the morning or later.

About that time, the girls would straggle in from the Casino. Having hoofed all evening, the young ladies were dog tired, and the last thing they wanted was, well, the last thing they wanted.

Just as some of the Chief's card-playing mates would begin to express, er, interest in the late arrivals, the Chief would suggest that all the Catholic lads in the crowd accompany him to 2:00 A.M. mass, the so-called printer's mass. He was a most persuasive fellow, this Rooney, especially in matters of religion, and soon he had a crowd marching off to mass—and away from temptation.

"The girls," Art Rooney, Jr., says, "loved it."

## MOTHER PIERRE'S WHOREHOUSE

Hall-of-Fame running back Johnny Blood McNally was the playboy of the pro football world in the twenties and thirties. He retired in 1939—from the NFL, that is—but his legend lives on.

According to *The Pro Football Chronicle* by Dan Daly and Bob O'Donnell, McNally once checked into the Packers huddle with a pass play from coach Curly Lambeau. He made the call, then turned to quarterback Arnie Herber and said: "Arnie, throw it in the direction of Mother Pierre's whorehouse."

Herber, no stranger to the Green Bay nightlife, knew McNally was heading for the goal post at the northeast end of the stadium. The pass was there; so was McNally.

When McNally first joined the Packers in 1929, he asked for a salary of $100 a game. Lambeau came back with an offer of $110 with the stipulation that he not drink past Tuesday of each week. "I countered with an offer to take the $100 I had proposed and drink through Wednesday," McNally said. "Curly agreed."

The Packers won their first title in '29, and the city held a banquet for the players. Each was presented a $220 check, a wallet, and a pocket watch.

**Sinew and Brawn, one writer called them: Bill Hewitt (left) and Bronko Nagurski during a preseason warm-up in the early thirties. The two helped make the Chicago Bears the dominant team of the era, with two NFL titles, 1932 and 1933, and a title-game loss in 1934. Hewitt, an end out of Michigan, played for the Bears from 1932 through 1936, and then played three more years with the Philadelphia Eagles. Nagurski, fullback on offense and tackle on defense, from Minnesota, starred for the Bears from 1930 through 1937, and then came back after a five-year layoff to help them win the NFL title in 1943.**

A sculpture worthy of Rodin: Steve Bagarus (No. 00) of the Washington Redskins and an unidentified pass defender.

McNally was the last to address the gathering of more than 400 and, after thanking the fans and Packers ownership, said: "I am especially grateful for the check."

## DEVOTED FANS

Ken Strong made his pro football debut with the Staten Island Stapletons in 1929 and played with them for four seasons before moving across New York Bay to join the Giants. He told this story from those days to author Bob Curran for his book *Pro Football's Rag Days:*

> **I'll give you an idea of what those Stape fans were like. During those years I developed a rivalry with Ray Flaherty, the Giants' captain. One day, when we were playing at Thompson Field, I went around his end and he grabbed me in a headlock. Right near one side of the field we had a small wire fence that was right against the sidelines. Now Flaherty started to force me towards the wire fence. And something was getting him real mad. When the whistle blew, he looked up and saw this little old lady leaning over the fence waving an umbrella. She'd been hitting him on the head while he was pulling me towards the sidelines and he thought that I had been reaching up and punching him.**

## CAREERS

Four of the most famous football names in the NFL's first college player draft, conducted in 1936, were Heisman Trophy winner Jay Berwanger of the University of Chicago, Notre Dame's triple-threat All-American back Bill Shakespeare, Alabama's rugged end Paul "Bear" Bryant, and All-American end Eddie Erdelatz of St. Mary's College. All four, however, declined to sign pro contracts, which in those days offered paltry salaries in the range of $125 to $250 per game for a top rookie, and opted for careers that at least at that time appeared more lucrative.

All four, however, declined to sign pro contracts, which in those days offered paltry salaries in the range of $125 to $250 per game for a top rookie . . .

## HIT HIM IN THE EYE

Ray Flaherty, who made it to the Hall of Fame as an end with the New York Giants, was also a fine head coach for the Washington Redskins from 1937 through 1942. The story of his first encounter with "Slingin'" Sammy Baugh, his rookie quarterback in 1937, is a classic.

At the team's first workout at summer camp, Flaherty wanted to see just how good a passer Baugh was. He told Wayne Millner, the Redskins' All-Pro end, to run a short pattern over the middle and buttonhook just behind the middle linebacker. Then he turned to Baugh, "I want you to hit him square in the eye with the ball," Flaherty said.

One of the New York Giants' most enduring greats, Ken Strong joined the team in 1933 after four years across the bay with the Staten Island Stapletons. An All-American from NYU, the triple-threat halfback played three years for the Giants, then jumped to the New York Yanks in the short-lived AFL, and then came back to the Giants in 1939. He then left for four years of military service during World War II, but returned for four more football years with the Giants from 1944 through 1947. Ball carrier, passer, punter, place-kicker, and outstanding defensive back, Strong was inducted into the Pro Football Hall of Fame in 1967.

"Sure, coach," the rangy 23-year-old Texan said and moved into his then-tailback position to take the snap from the center. Then Baugh looked over his shoulder at Flaherty and said, "One thing, coach. Which eye?"

## LARGE SCUFFLES, LARGE PAINS

Was it a rugged game, the one they played back in the thirties? Consider this account from the *New York Times* of the 1938 NFL championship game between the New York Giants and the Green Bay Packers:

> What a frenzied battle this was! The tackling was fierce and the blocking positively vicious. In the last drive every scrimmage pile-up saw a Packer tackler stretched on the ground. . . . As for the Giants, they really were hammered to a fare-thee-well.
>
> Johnny Dell Isola was taken to St. Elizabeth's hospital with a spinal concussion that just missed being a fractured vertebra. Ward Cuff suffered a possible fracture of the sternum.
>
> Mel Hein, kicked in the cheekbone at the end of the second quarter, suffered a concussion of the brain that left him temporarily bereft of his memory. He came in to the final quarter and finished the game. Leland Shaffer sustained a badly sprained ankle.
>
> The play for the full sixty vibrant minutes was absolutely ferocious. No such blocking and tackling by two football teams ever had been seen at the Polo Grounds. Tempers were so frayed and tattered that stray punches were tossed around all afternoon. This was the gridiron sport at its primitive best.

**With the franchise for 16 years, Sammy Baugh was synonymous with the Washington Redskins. The All-Pro single-wing tailback who would convert to an All-Pro T-formation quarterback in the forties joined the Redskins in 1937 after a great college career at Texas Christian University. When he retired after the 1952 season, he owned NFL career passing records for completions, attempts, yardage, touchdowns, and completion percentage as well as various punting standards. He was a charter enshrinee in the Pro Football Hall of Fame in 1963.**

"One of the Bears' players went over to the sideline and told George Halas that we were wearing sneakers. 'Step on their toes,' Halas shouted to his players."

—GIANTS OWNER
WELLINGTON MARA

The Giants, incidentally, won the game, 23–17, with the winning touchdown coming on a pass from Ed Danowski to Hank Soar.

### SNEAKERS, ABE COHEN, AND A CHAMPIONSHIP

Hero of the New York Giants' first triumph in an NFL title game, the "sneakers" championship of 1934, was 5'2", 140-pound Abe Cohen, who wasn't even a player. Giants' owner Wellington Mara told of how Cohen achieved his immortality:

At the Polo Grounds on Sunday morning, the field was completely frozen. We had a little fellow on the payroll named Abe Cohen, a sort of jack-of-all-trades. Abe was a tailor by profession, and he also worked for Chick Meehan, who was a famous coach at Manhattan College and was quite a showman in his own way. Meehan was the first coach to put what we call satin pants on a football team. He had done that first at NYU in the days of Ken Strong. Abe was his tailor and made the pants for the players so that they would fit properly. [Coach] Steven Owen asked Abe to go up to Manhattan College, to which he had access—he had a key to their equipment room

Redskins' end Wayne Millner (No. 40), on defense here, joined the team in Boston in 1936 after an All-American college career at Notre Dame. His seven-year stint with the Redskins was interrupted by three wartime years of military service. A key receiver (he caught two touchdown passes in the 1937 NFL title game, which the Redskins won), he was also a great blocker and defensive end. Millner entered the Pro Football Hall of Fame in 1968.

and the gym—and borrow the sneakers from the lockers of the basketball players and bring them over to the Polo Grounds for our players.

Abe got in a taxi and went to Manhattan. I think he had to break into the lockers. At any rate he got back around halftime of the game with nine or ten pairs of sneakers.

Some of the players didn't want to put them on, but those who did had so much success that eventually most of our players put them on. Ken Strong, who kicked off for us, placekicked with the sneakers on, and he lost a toenail on his big toe. In the second half we began moving the ball. One of the Bears' players went over to the sideline and told George Halas that we were wearing sneakers. "Step on their toes," Halas shouted to his players.

The following week after the championship—in those days you had barnstorming trips after the season was over—the Bears were playing an exhibition game in Philadelphia, and Steve Owen and I went down to see the game. We went into the Bears' dressing room, I guess to crow a little bit, and the first thing we saw was about 24 pairs of sneakers on top of the lockers. Halas said to us, "I'll never get caught like that again."

The Giants' first great running back, Alphonse "Tuffy" Leemans, from George Washington University, carries the ball here in a game against the Green Bay Packers in the late thirties. Leemans starred for the Giants for eight years as a premier ball carrier (he led the league in rushing his rookie year with 830 yards), passer, and pass receiver. He was elected to the Pro Football Hall of Fame in 1978.

And as for Abe Cohen, Lewis Burton summed it up best in the December 10, 1934, edition of the *New York American:* "To the heroes of antiquity, to the Greek who raced across the Marathon plain, and to Paul Revere, add now the name of Abe Cohen."

## A NOVEL FORM OF BANKING

In the book *Lions Pride*, which commemorated the Detroit Lions' 60th anniversary (they were founded in 1934), there was this little slice of what life was like when the game of professional football was young:

> During the early days . . . the sport was unstable and its future was uncertain, at best. It wasn't always known where the money was going to come from, and players insisted on being paid before they played. Former Detroit coach Alvin "Bo" McMillin liked to tell the story of the day he played in Milwaukee [1922] and was upset by a hard tackle.
>
> "The boys looked down at me and figured I'd broken my leg," said McMillin. "There was a big bulge on my leg and it looked like the bone was sticking right out. It wasn't, though. I'd been paid with 100-dollar bills. I was afraid to leave it in the clubhouse, so I stuck it down my stocking."

**Mel Hein was the NFL All-Pro center for eight consecutive years (1933–40). After leaving Washington State, he played for the New York Giants for 15 years (1931–45), never missed a game, and played 60 minutes in most of them. He is a charter member of the Pro Football Hall of Fame, enshrined in 1963.**

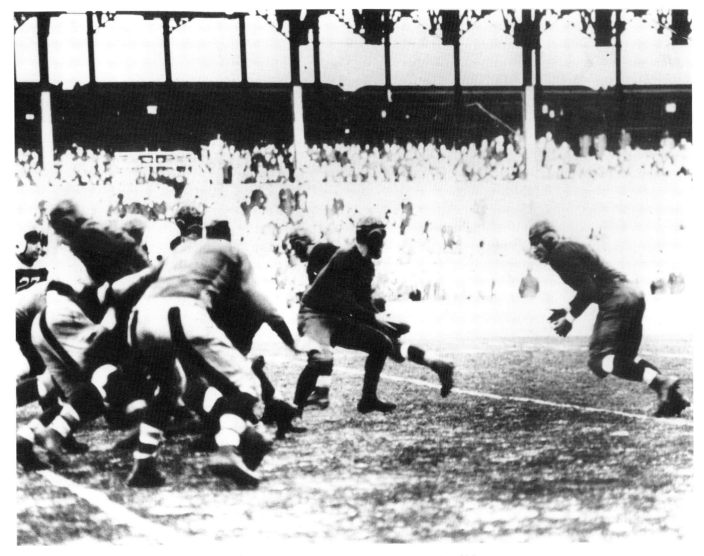

A scene from the 1934 NFL title game between the New York Giants and the Chicago Bears, better known as the "Sneakers" championship. Here, Bronko Nagurski is about to take a lateral from Bears quarterback Carl Brumbaugh, but the mighty Nagurski could not that day overcome Mother Nature, who provided a treacherously slippery field. The Giants prevailed by switching their football cleats to sneakers for the second half and turning a halftime deficit of 10–3 into a 30–13 victory (New York scored 27 points in the fourth quarter).

A seemingly unreal scene: Jim Brown (No. 32) performing in a near-empty stadium in 1960. But the game between the Browns and the Cowboys was in Dallas, and the Cowboys were in their first, shaky year in the NFL. Brown went on to lead the league in rushing that year (1,257 yards, a 5.6 average), while the Cowboys suffered through a 0–11–1 season. Cleveland won this game 48–7. On the ground is Cleveland's Ray Renfro; the Cowboy with hopes of tackling Brown is Tom Franckhauser.

**2**

Curious
Insights

FROM A COLUMN IN *THE DALLAS MORNING NEWS* BY BOB ST. JOHN

"When the One Great Scorer comes
to write against your name—
He marks—not that you won or lost
—but how you played the game."

—GRANTLAND RICE

"Bull."

—TEX SCHRAMM

**O**ne thing that can be said about the game of professional football, by any who have played it, coached it, or covered it for the media, is that just when you think it's going to be predictable, it isn't. Momentum changes, costly goof-ups occur, or a seemingly superhuman effort comes to pass. Upsets are not uncommon; players come off the bench to astound fans with their unexpected performances; strange things just happen on a football field.

But there are the constants.

There have been the truly great players: running backs from Red Grange to Emmitt Smith, quarterbacks from Sammy Baugh to Brett Favre, pass catchers from Don Hutson to Jerry Rice, as well as great defenders, great blockers, and great special-teams players. There have also been the dynasties. The Chicago Bears of the early thirties played in three consecutive NFL title games and won two of them with stars like Grange, Bronko Nagurski, and Bill Hewitt. The Green Bay Packers ruled the second half of that decade, also appearing in three championship matches and prevailing in two of them; their legends included Hutson, Clarke Hinkle, Arnie Herber, and Cecil Isbell.

Then there were the Bears of the forties, with such luminaries as Sid Luckman, George McAfee, Bulldog Turner, Ken Kavanaugh, and Danny Fortmann. In the fifties, it was the Cleveland Browns, coming over from the old All-America Football Conference (AAFC), with a roster of Hall of Famers that included Otto Graham, Marion Motley, Dante Lavelli, Lou Groza, and Bill Willis, and the Detroit Lions (the two teams met in three straight NFL title games—1952–54—the Lions winning two of them), who boasted of such greats as Bobby Layne, Doak Walker, Leon Hart, and Lou Creekmur.

The sixties and early seventies saw the launch of the American Football League, the merger with the NFL, and the introduction of the Super Bowl. It was also the heart of the Lombardi era in Green Bay with the Packers winning five NFL championships, including the first Super Bowl; their list of stars glittered with names like Paul Hornung, Bart Starr, Jim Taylor, Boyd Dowler, Forrest Gregg, Ray Nitschke, Willie Davis, Herb Adderley, and Willie Wood.

Following the Pack were the Dallas Cowboys, who became known as "America's Team" because of their national following of fans. They had quarterbacks like Don

**Norm Van Brocklin, who quarterbacked at Oregon before coming to the NFL in 1949, spent nine years with the Los Angeles Rams and his last three in Philadelphia with the Eagles. Known as the "Dutchman," he was one of the game's best passers, field generals, and punters. He went on to become head coach of the Minnesota Vikings (1961–66) and the Atlanta Falcons (1968–74). The Dutchman entered the Pro Football Hall of Fame in 1971.**

Meredith and Roger Staubach and other memorable performers such as Bob Hayes, Bob Lilly, Chuck Howley, Lee Roy Jordan, and Drew Pearson. Then along came the Pittsburgh Steelers, winners of Super Bowls IX, X, XIII, and XIV, with their litany of legends: Terry Bradshaw, Franco Harris, Lynn Swann, John Stallworth, "Mean" Joe Greene, and Jack Lambert.

There have also been the San Francisco 49ers, led by Joe Montana; the Washington Redskins in the era of Joe Gibbs; John Elway guiding the Denver Broncos; and the forever also-rans known as the Buffalo Bills (four AFC titles in those years, but four consecutive losses in Super Bowls XXV–XXVIII).

And, of course, there was the only team ever to go undefeated, the Miami Dolphins of 1972 (17–0–0), capping it triumphantly with a victory in Super Bowl VII, behind such stars as Bob Griese, Paul Warfield, Larry Csonka, Jim Kiick, and Nick Buoniconti.

Mixed in with all that greatness are some very interesting incidents, oddball moments, and behind-the-scenes happenings that are equally worth remembering. Curious insights they are.

### PINPOINT PASSING

Quarterbacks do not *always* aim to complete a pass. Corroboration of this came from Art Donovan, the Colts' great defensive tackle of the fifties:

> "I gave him a little elbow . . . just to show him a quarterback shouldn't make threats to a defensive tackle."
>
> —ART DONOVAN

Norm Van Brocklin of the Rams was a tough quarterback; he'd hang in there taking all you had. Once, after I'd laid him low with one particularly vicious sack, he turned to me and said, "You hit me like that again and I'm gonna get your big fat ass." I soon got him again, and I gave him a little elbow while we were rolling around on the ground, just to show him a quarterback shouldn't make threats to a defensive tackle. Well, on the next play the offensive lineman in front of me just stepped out of they way. I didn't know what was going on. I had a clear path to the quarterback. But before I knew what hit me, Van Brocklin fired a line drive as hard as he could right into my face. But boy, it knocked me flat on my ass. I couldn't believe that he'd just waste a play like that. I guess he was mad. You have to have respect for a guy like that.

### ON THORPE

Chicago Bears end/coach/owner George Halas on Jim Thorpe:

To have Jim Thorpe tackle you from behind was an experience you couldn't forget. He wouldn't actually tackle you. With his great speed he'd run you down and then throw his huge body crosswise into your back. It was like having a redwood tree fall on you.

New York Giants tackle/coach Steve Owen on Thorpe:

I was playing for the Oklahoma All-Stars in 1923, fresh out of college, and we went up against a team that had Thorpe. He had lost some of his speed and power by that time, I'd been told. On the first play that I was on defense, I broke through into the backfield and charged into Thorpe, who was blocking. I shoved a hand into his face and knocked him down. On the next play I did the same thing and thought, Old Jim really has slowed down. Then on the next play I kind of ignored him and went straight for the ball carrier. Suddenly I thought the whole grandstand had fallen on me. I went down, stunned and shaken. When I finally got back up, I realized Thorpe had blocked me. He patted me on the back and said, "Always keep an eye on an old Indian!"

## HUT, HUT . . . *UN, DEUX, TROIS*

George Eddy, commentator for French television at Super Bowl XXVI:

Many [French] don't understand certain elements of it [American football]. Soccer and rugby are our most popular sports, and they have continuous action. So some of our fans don't know why football players have to stop and talk after each play. They ask, "Why don't the Americans just pick up the ball and run when the referee puts it down?"

## WASHINGTON *"ROTHAEUTE"*

The *Frankfurter Allgemeine* newspaper in Germany, in its Super Bowl XXVI coverage, tried to describe the Washington *Rothaeute* (German for Redskins) to its readers by comparing them to "an oversized agricultural machine" that "systematically mows" the field. And here we thought they were just the Hogs.

Jim Thorpe was the biggest name in football, at least until Red Grange showed up at Illinois in 1923. Thorpe was a star at Carlisle Institute under legendary coach Pop Warner before becoming a pro (which happened before the NFL was founded in 1920) and an Olympic legend (1912). The Sac and Fox American Indian was the heart of the Canton Bulldogs in the league's first year. Thorpe also played for the Cleveland Indians, Oorang Indians, Toledo Maroons, Rock Island Independents, New York Giants, and Chicago Cardinals in the twenties. He was a charter inductee of the Pro Football Hall of Fame in 1963.

### AND THAT'S THE TRUTH

Washington Redskins' quarterback Doug Williams was asked by a reporter at a press conference before Super Bowl XXII, "How long have you been a black quarterback?"

The "Hogs" in action. In the thick of this human riot is the offensive line of the Washington Redskins of the early eighties, doing combat with the New York Giants. Given the nickname by offensive line coach Joe Bugel, the original Hogs were tackles Joe Jacoby and George Starke, guards Russ Grimm and Mark May, and center Jeff Bostic, joined by subsequent offensive linemen Raleigh McKenzie, Ed Simmons, Mark Schlereth, and Jim Lachey. Running back John Riggins was later awarded honorary "Hog" status.

**A close-up in the "Hog" pen. Tackle Joe Jacoby takes on a New York Jet in a true face-to-face confrontation.**

His response: "I've been a quarterback since high school; I've always been black."

## THE PRESIDENTS SPEAK

Don Shula, head coach of the Miami Dolphins, was at home watching a film of his team's victory over the Baltimore Colts for the 1971 AFC championship (which earned for them the right to meet the Dallas Cowboys in Super Bowl VI). It was 1:30 in the morning, and he was surprised when the telephone rang.

"Mr. Shula, please," the voice at the other end said when he answered it.

"Yeah, speaking."

"The president is calling."

And suddenly there was the familiar voice of Richard M. Nixon. After they exchanged pleasantries, the president said: "Now you understand that I'm a Washington Redskins fan, but I'm a part-time resident of Miami [referring to his winter home at Key Biscayne], and I've been following the Dolphins real close, Don. Now the Cowboys are a good football team, but I still think you can hit Warfield on that down-and-in pattern against them. You know the one."

"Now the Cowboys are a good football team, but I still think you can hit Warfield on that down-and-in pattern against them. You know the one."

—RICHARD M. NIXON

A few days later, Tom Landry received a telegram from Austin, Texas. It was from former President Lyndon B. Johnson. It read, "Tom, my prayers and my presence will be with you in New Orleans, although I have no plans to send in any plays." —Lyndon B. Johnson

After the game (the Cowboys won 24–3), Tom Landry was handed a telephone in the winners' locker room. It was a call from President Nixon. When the brief conversation was over, Landry showed the trace of a smile: "He complimented us on playing almost perfect football," he said to the writers and broadcasters flocked around him, "especially our offensive line."

One sportswriter asked quickly, "Did he mention anything about the down-and-in to Warfield?" The flicker of a smile once again crossed Landry's face. "No, that never came up."

### MICHELANGELO AND WHO?

Washington coach Joe Gibbs was asked by a sports reporter if he should be labeled a football genius following his third Super Bowl (XXVI) victory in 1992.

His response: "As Mr. Cooke [Redskins owner Jack Kent Cooke] says, 'There have been only two [geniuses] in history, and none of them has been in football. Michelangelo was one of them and I forget who the other was.'"

**The age of exhibition games. They were very much a part of the National Football League all the way through the fifties.**

A youthful George Blanda poses here as a member of the Chicago Bears, the team he joined at age 21 in 1949. He hung up his cleats at age 48 in 1975 as an Oakland Raider, with interim stints as a Baltimore Colt and a Houston Oiler. A quarterback and placekicker, he held the NFL career scoring record when he finally retired. Blanda was elected to the Pro Football Hall of Fame in 1981.

## THE MORNING AFTER

Here are some thoughts and comments after the carnage, better known as the NFL championship game of 1940, in which the Chicago Bears annihilated the Washington Redskins 73–0, which remains the largest margin of defeat ever in any NFL regular-season or postseason game.

Sammy Baugh, when asked if the outcome might have been different had Redskins end Charley Malone caught what appeared to be a touchdown pass in the first quarter with the score a mere 7–0, Bears: "Hell, yes, the score would have been 73–6."

Bob Considine, in his syndicated sports column, "On the Line": "The Chicago Bears massacred the Washington Redskins 73–0 yesterday. . . . The unluckiest guy in the crowd was the five-buck bettor who took the Redskins and 70 points."

Shirley Povich, in his column "This Morning" for the *Washington Post:* "If you're wanting to know what happened to the Redskins yesterday, maybe this will explain it: The Bears happened to 'em. . . . It reminds us of our first breathless visit

**Redskins quarterback Doug Williams (No. 17) unloads a pass. A Grambling graduate, Williams led the Skins to Super Bowl XXII, where they defeated the Denver Broncos 42–10; with four Super Bowl records and four touchdown passes in the game, he was named that year's Super Bowl MVP.**

to the Grand Canyon. All we could say is: 'There she is, and ain't she a beaut.' When they hung up that final score at Griffith Stadium yesterday, all we could utter was: 'There it is, and wasn't it awful.'"

Bill Stern, sports broadcaster: "It got so bad that, toward the end, the Bears had to give up placekicking the extra points and try passes instead because all the footballs booted into the stands were being kept by the spectators as souvenirs. And they were down to their last football."

Red Smith, in his column "Sports of the Times" for *The New York Times:* "George Preston Marshall, the mettlesome laundryman who owned the Redskins, looked on from the stands—except when he turned his back to charge up the aisle and throw a punch at a dissatisfied customer—and when his ordeal was over, every hair in his raccoon coat had turned white."

Redskins owner Marshall at a press conference after the game: "We were awful and you don't need to ask me if we are going to clean house. Some of the boys are going to be embarrassed when the time comes to make contracts for next year."

### PRIORITIES

The late Jack Mara, former president of the New York Giants football team, often told the story of George Preston Marshall and his football priorities.

The Giants were in Washington one year in the mid-forties to play the Redskins when a freak snowstorm left the field under about a foot of snow. An hour before the teams were to take the field for pregame warm-ups, Mara was surveying the situation from the sideline, wondering if indeed it would be possible to play a game in all that snow.

The Way It Was . . .

...on Dec. 24, 1950, when QB Otto Graham led the Cleveland Browns to their first NFL championship over the high scoring Los Angeles Rams in a 30-28 thriller !

with Curt Gowdy

LOU GROZA kicked the winning 16-yard field goal !

ELROY HIRSCH of the Rams

OTTO GRAHAM

His thoughts were interrupted, however, when he saw Marshall trudging across the field in the knee-high snow. As he approached, Marshall shook his head. "Don't worry, Jack, they're coming," he said. "They'll be here in plenty of time."

"Snowplows?" Mara asked.

"Snowplows, hell," Marshall said with a look of great disbelief. "I'm talking about overshoes for the band."

### PENDING EVACUATION

Chicago Bears executive Michael McCaskey, grandson of George Halas, grew up with the Bears, even practiced with them in the summers when he played end for Yale in the sixties. He had a number of curious insights collected over the years, none more amusing than those involving the legendary defensive end Doug Atkins:

**A youthful Don Shula, on the sideline for the Miami Dolphins. After seven years as head coach of the Baltimore Colts, Shula guided Miami's destiny from 1970 to 1995. During his distinguished coaching career, Shula took the Colts to one Super Bowl (III) and Miami to five others, winning two of them (VII and VIII). When he retired from the game, Shula was the winningest coach in NFL history, with an overall record of 347–173–6. He was inducted into the Pro Football Hall of Fame in 1997.**

Doug battled the weight thing all the time. Different players had different ways of getting the weight off. Rick Casares, for example, would go to a sauna and sweat it off. Atkins, however, found a unique approach one year. Wednesday ordinarily was the weigh-in day, and Doug walked up to my grandfather on one Tuesday, and he had one of those big paper cups filled with Ex-Lax. He said, "Coach, is there gonna be a weigh-in tomorrow?"

Halas looked at him and said, "Tomorrow's Wednesday, isn't it?"

Then Doug, right in front of him, downed this enormous cup of Ex-Lax.

My grandfather stared at him all the way through it, and when Doug finished chewing, he looked away from Doug and announced to the rest, "No weigh-in tomorrow."

## IMAGE CONSCIOUS

Dallas Cowboys quarterback Roger Staubach said this on his image as the clean-cut, All-American boy:

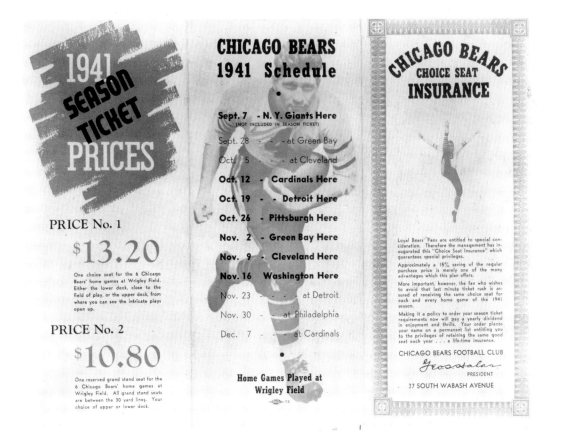

**Season ticket prices, 1941.**

I'm not happy with the way the press treats me. . . . It's gotten to the point where I can't say something in jest without being taken seriously. I once went to pick up my kid's dog at the vet and it wound up in print like it was my favorite pastime. Hell, I didn't even like the dog.

## FETID FIELD OF PLAY

The field of play in the NFL was not always elysian, as Art Donovan, the Colts' colorful defensive lineman during the fifties, recalled in his autobiography *Fatso*:

Sophistication was not exactly a hallmark of the early NFL. We were like barnstormers, and we were treated as such. The Colts played the Giants once in an exhibition game in Louisville. It was a brand-new stadium, and the first thing they had in there was the circus. Unfortunately, the Colts and the Giants were the second thing they had in there.

Redskins head coach Joe Gibbs confers with his muddied quarterback, Jay Schroeder, during a game. Gibbs, in command from 1981 through 1992, is Washington's all-time winningest coach (124–60–0 in the regular season and 16–5 in the postseason).

Every time you put your hand down, you stuck it into a pile of elephant shit. But that was OK for us. We were on the defensive line. It was the offensive linemen who were getting the worst of it. Every time the Giants offense set, and their linemen couldn't move, we'd pick up gobs of this shit and throw it in their faces. They were screaming and hollering all day about this indignity, but the officials were at a loss. "Sorry, boys," they'd say. "They can move. They're allowed to move. But after you get into your three-point stance, you guys have to stay still."

Right near the end of the game, an offensive guard for the Giants by the name of Jack Stroud had had enough. He came up to the line of scrimmage, bent down, picked up a fistful of this muck, yelled, "You dirty sonsabitches!" and threw it at us. He got called for a five-yard penalty for being in motion.

## MONTANA'S GREATEST GAME

When famed Oakland Raiders coach and later more famous pro football television commentator John Madden was asked which was the greatest of the many fabulous performances Joe Montana put on in an NFL game, he responded:

**The battle of the quarterbacks, Sammy Baugh and Sid Luckman, in the NFL championship game of 1940. It turned into the most one-sided battle in NFL history as the Bears annihilated the Redskins 73–0, still the largest margin of victory in any NFL game.**

Doug Atkins, a world-class defensive end out of Tennessee, came to the Chicago Bears from the Cleveland Browns (1953–54), allegedly because Paul Brown could not control him. George Halas could—sort of—as it turned out, and Atkins stayed around for 12 seasons (1955–66) before finishing out his Hall of Fame career with the New Orleans Saints (1967–69). At 6'8" and 275 pounds and with an attitude, Atkins struck fear in the hearts of teammates as well as opponents. He was inducted into the Pro Football Hall of Fame in 1982.

I can pick only one.

I could've picked a dozen, maybe more, starting with the 49ers' 20–16 win over the Bengals in Super Bowl XXIII when Joe hit John Taylor for a 10-yard touchdown with 34 seconds left. Or the 1981 NFC championship game against the Cowboys when his six-yard pass to Dwight Clark with 51 seconds left put the 49ers into Super Bowl XVI. Or his five touchdown passes in the 55–10 rout of the Broncos in Super Bowl XXIV. Or anytime the 49ers were behind in the fourth quarter. The more pressure, the better he was. When he was behind, he always knew he was going to beat you. His teammates knew. The fans knew. And when he really had you was when the other team knew. But as great as he was in all those games for the 49ers, I picked another game.

[But the greatest!] His game for the Chiefs against the 49ers. Joe had been traded to the Chiefs in 1993 but they lost the AFC championship game in Buffalo after he suffered a concussion. When the 1994 season began, it was probably his last time around. The second weekend, the Chiefs were playing the 49ers in Kansas City, the old gunslinger against his old teammates. He had the inferior team, but he was just about perfect. He hit 19 of 31 passes for 206 yards and two touchdowns with no interceptions as the Chiefs won, 24–14, over the 49ers team that would go on to win Super Bowl XXIX.

## OFF THE BENCH

Here's a piece of Pittsburgh Steelers lore from *The Pittsuburg Steelers* by Abby Mendelson:

At halftime of the final game of the dismal 4–7–1 1951 campaign, the Steelers found themselves in an accustomed position—trailing somebody, this time the Skins, 10–0. With all hope gone, coach John Michelosen turned to Tulsa's Jim Finks and converted him from defensive back to quarterback.

"Can you help us, son?" Michelosen pleaded.

"Sure," Finks nodded.

On the icy field, with no practice at offense, Finks pulled off what may be the greatest sustained surprise in Steelers history—three second-half touchdown passes to net a 20–10 victory.

The team was jubilant, but the Chief [Art Rooney] fired Michelosen anyway.

But the Steelers had a quarterback for the next four years. When he retired after the '55 season, Finks had passed for 8,854 yards, good for fifth place on the all-time team list.

A number of pro football stars of the sixties served in the military reserves, as recorded here by cartoonist Murray Olderman.

JUST A HELMET LINER NOW

BOBBY MITCHELL    PAUL HORNUNG

SERVICE CALLS

Frank Gifford, an All-American from Southern Cal, was drafted by the New York Giants in 1952 and hung around the Big Apple for a 12-year football career (missing the 1961 season because of an injury) and a long television broadcasting career after it was over. Playing halfback and later flanker, he was an All-Pro four times (1955, 1956, 1957, and 1959) and was invited to seven Pro Bowls. Gifford earned his way into the Pro Football Hall of Fame in 1977.

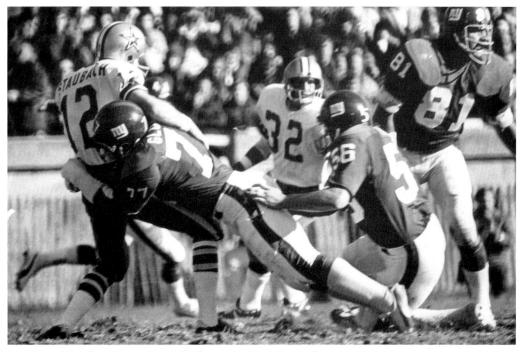

**Leader of the Cowboys through the seventies, Roger Staubach, taking a rather inglorious hit here from Giants pass rusher Rich Glover, came to Dallas after an All-American career at Navy and four years' active duty in, among other places, Vietnam. A 27-year-old rookie, he became the team's greatest quarterback, renowned not only for his passing and leadership on the field but also as one of the greatest comeback quarterbacks in the history of the game. When he retired after the 1979 season, Staubach was the NFL's all-time passing leader. He was enshrined in the Pro Football Hall of Fame in 1985.**

### DENTAL OBSERVATION

The Rams had just been routed 56–20 in a 1950 game against Philadelphia. Los Angeles head coach Joe Stydahar stormed into the dressing room and started to roar at his players. "No wonder you guys got kicked around," he fumed. "Every guy on the team has still got all his teeth."

### ON GALE SAYERS

One of the most dazzling runners in the history of the National Football League was Chicago Bears halfback Gale Sayers. Besides running from scrimmage, he returned kickoffs and punts and set or tied NFL records in all three categories during his all-too-brief career in the NFL. His spectacular performances were enough, however, to earn him admission into pro football's Hall of Fame and were corroborated by two who played against him.

"I hit him so hard near the line of scrimmage I thought my shoulder must have busted him in two."

—RAMS DEFENSIVE TACKLE
ROSEY GRIER

Here's what Rosey Grier, a Rams defensive tackle in 1965, had to say about him:

I hit him so hard near the line of scrimmage I thought my shoulder must have busted him in two. I heard a roar from the crowd and figured he must have fumbled. I was on the ground and when I looked up he was 15 yards down the field and going for the score.

And, this from George Donnelly, 49ers defensive back:

He looks no different than any other runner when he's coming at you, but when he gets there, he's gone.

## FROZEN IN TIME

When the Packers hosted the Cowboys for the NFL championship game of 1967, the temperature was -13, with 15-mile-an-hour winds whipping around Lambeau Field. The game, which the Packers won 21–17 on a quarterback sneak by Bart Starr with 13 seconds left, became known forever after as the "Ice Bowl." Here are some comments on that day in Green Bay as recorded in *The Pro Football Chronicle* by Dan Daly and Bob O'Donnell.

Don Meredith, Dallas quarterback that day: "All I have to say is, there was trouble on every corner."

Lance Rentzel, Dallas wide receiver, on his wake-up call that morning: "Good morning, Mr. Rentzel. It's 8:00 A.M. It's 15 below zero, and there's a 20-mile-per-hour wind coming out of the northwest. Have a nice day."

Jim Murray, from his column in the *Los Angeles Times*: "I don't know why they scheduled this game here—I guess because the top of Mt. Everest was booked."

**Jim Finks, coming out of Tulsa, was a fine quarterback for the Pittsburgh Steelers from 1949 to 1955. His biggest contributions to the National Football League, however, came as an administrator, first at Minnesota, where he put together teams that went to four Super Bowls, then with the Chicago Bears, where he assembled the team that won Super Bowl XX. He finished out his administrative career with the New Orleans Saints. Finks was elected to the Pro Football Hall of Fame in 1995.**

**Green Bay great Jim Taylor, a product of Louisiana State University, roars through a huge hole in the Colts' defense. One of the most powerful fullbacks in history, Taylor rounded out the great Packers backfield that featured halfback Paul Hornung and quarterback Bart Starr in Vince Lombardi's Green Bay dynasty of the sixties. He rushed for more than 1,000 yards in five consecutive seasons (1960–64) and was a punishing blocker when he wasn't carrying the ball. Taylor joined the Pro Football Hall of Fame in 1976.**

Clint Murchison, Cowboys owner: "If I owned Green Bay, I'd dome the whole town."

Frank Gifford, announcing the game on television that day: "I think I'll have another bite of my coffee."

Dan Reeves, Dallas running back: "You hear that stuff about the Packers being able to deal with [the weather] better than we did, and that's a lot of bull. I think we handled it as well as they did. It's just that they made the play at the end."

Lionel Aldridge, Packers defensive end: "It was so cold that winning wasn't uppermost in my mind. Getting out of the weather was."

Chuck Mercein, Packers running back: "Falling on that ground was like falling on the side of a stucco wall. It made AstroTurf feel like a pillow."

Tom Landry, Cowboys coach: "It was kind of an eerie feeling. I was standing there on the sidelines, and I'd look around and there'd be nobody. Everyone would

"Falling on that ground was like falling on the side of a stucco wall. It made AstroTurf feel like a pillow."

—PACKERS RUNNING BACK CHUCK MERCEIN

The "Kansas Comet" was the nick-name Gale Sayers brought with him when he was drafted by the Chicago Bears in 1965 (along with Dick Butkus in one of the greatest first-round draft tandem selections ever in the NFL). He illustrated his astronomical dazzle the very first year, setting a then-NFL record of 22 touchdowns and tying another when he scored 6 in a single game against the 49ers. Regarded as per-haps the greatest open-field runner the game has ever seen, Sayers, in a seven-year career shortened by knee injuries, gained the distinc-tion of becoming the youngest player ever to enter the Pro Football Hall of Fame when he was inducted in 1977.

be back at the heaters trying to stay warm. I was all by myself, just like I was up at the North Pole. It was the kind of feeling where you wonder what you're doing here and why this thing wasn't called off."

Bob Skoronski, Green Bay offensive tackle: "This game was our mark of distinction."

"Kicking to Grange is like grooving one to Babe Ruth."

—CHICAGO CARDINALS
PUNTER PADDY DRISCOLL

### KICKING TO GRANGE

Red Grange made his pro football debut on Thanksgiving Day 1925, playing for the Chicago Bears against their crosstown rival, the Cardinals. The game ended in a scoreless tie. Grange not only was held to 36 yards rushing but he was unable to exercise one of his other notorious threats, returning punts.

The Cardinals' triple-threat tailback Paddy Driscoll punted many times that day, but he always kept it away from Grange, kicking either to Joey Sternaman or out of bounds. "Kicking to Grange," Driscoll said, "is like grooving one to Babe Ruth."

**Don Meredith was much better known as a passer for the Dallas Cowboys, but on occasion he ran the ball, as evidenced here in a game against the New York Giants. "Dandy Don," as he came to be known, from Southern Methodist University, quarterbacked the Cowboys through the dismal years (1960–64) and into the very good years when they became a championship contender in the second half of the sixties. Meredith then went on to a memorable career as a broadcaster on *Monday Night Football*, partnering with Howard Cosell and Frank Gifford. Cowboy No. 62 is guard Leon Donohue.**

After the game was over and Grange had made his uneventful debut, Driscoll stopped at the seats behind the Cardinals bench to talk to his wife. As the other players headed for the locker room, there was a lot of booing. "I hate to hear the fans boo a young man like Grange," Driscoll said. "It wasn't his fault he couldn't break one today."

"Don't feel sorry for Grange," his wife said. "It's you they're booing."

## THE FIRST TV GAME

Jim Campbell, author and pro football historian, wrote this of the first pro football game ever televised:

> It was October 22, 1939 . . . The Philadelphia Eagles versus the Brooklyn Dodgers.
>
> The game was played in Brooklyn's Ebbets Field before 13,000. . . . The Dodgers, with the help of three 40-yard-plus field goals by Ralph Kercheval, subdued the Eagles, 23–14. Two records were established that day—Kercheval's 45-yard field goal was the season's longest, and 6-foot, 205-pound Brooklyn fullback Ace Gutowsky eclipsed Cliff Battles' lifetime rushing mark when a brief appearance netted him 7

The "Galloping Ghost" (so pegged by sportswriter Grantland Rice): Red Grange carries the rounder football of the mid twenties in this photo. Grange, a legendary halfback in college at Illinois, joined the Chicago Bears in 1925. The barnstorming tour that ensued firmly established professional football in America, a direct result of Grange's appearances in cities throughout the nation. After a brief interlude in the American Football League, which he helped start (and where he injured his knee and as a result was never the dazzling runner he once had been), he returned to the Bears, still a first-rate halfback and one of the finest defensive backs in the game. Grange retired after the 1934 season and was named a charter member of the Pro Football Hall of Fame in 1963.

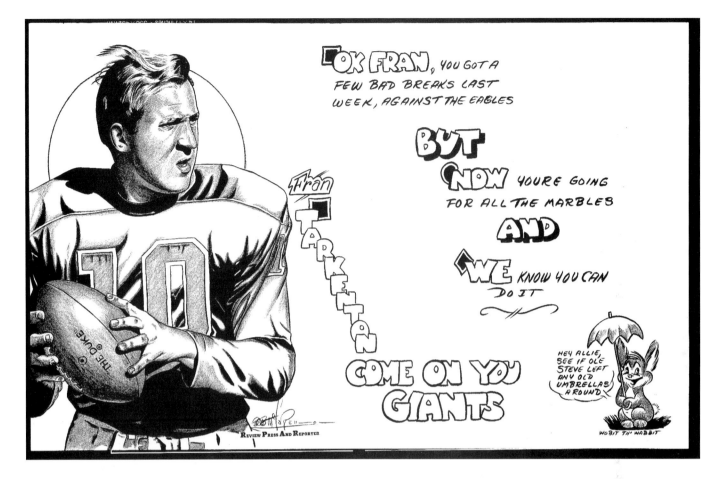

yards for a new standard of 3,399 yards. Pug Manders and Ace Parker also were Dodger standouts. . . .

For the Eagles, coached by Bert Bell, back Franny Murray ran and passed well all day and scored on a short sweep. Bill Hewitt, playing without a helmet, caught a six-point pass from 5-foot 7-inch, 150-pound Philly back Davey O'Brien.

But so far as anyone can tell, none of the players knew the game was being broadcast to the approximately one thousand TV sets in New York City.

"I didn't know about it," says Ace Parker today. Bruiser Kinard, Brooklyn's outstanding tackle, agreed: "I certainly wasn't aware of it."

The announcer for the game was Allan Walz, a former New York City Golden Gloves Champion and NYU football star who did the sports for (the NBC station) W2XBS.

"I remember the game," said Walz. "Pro football was a great game to do by television. . . . It was late in October on a cloudy day and when the sun crept behind the stadium there wasn't enough light for the cameras. The picture got darker and darker and eventually it went completely blank and we reverted to a radio broadcast. . . .

"We used two iconoscope cameras. I'd sit with my chin on the rail in the mezzanine and the camera would be over my shoulder. I did my own spotting and when the play moved up and down the field, on punts and kickoffs, I'd point to tell the cameraman what I'd been talking about and we used hand signals to communicate. The other camera was on the field, at the 50-yard line, but it couldn't move so we didn't use it much.

"Producer and director Burke Crotty was in the mobile unit truck and he'd tell me over the headphones which camera he was using. There wasn't a monitor up in the broadcasting box, but there was one on the field. I never really understood what that was for, but I think Potsy Clark [Brooklyn's coach] insisted on it. He was experimenting with scouting by television, I think.

"Afterwards, I'd interview players, but it was too dark by then to do television and the players probably thought I was just another of the radio men there."

Pat Summerall's fabled field goal in the snow, 1958, against the Cleveland Browns. No one knows exactly how long the kick was because of the blanket of snow, but it was at least a 49-yarder, and teammate Kyle Rote claimed it was 56 yards. Whatever the distance, it was one of the great clutch kicks in NFL lore, winning the game for the Giants, clinching a tie for the NFL East crown, and, of course, enabling them to participate in the sudden-death overtime championship game of 1958 with the Colts, often cited as the greatest game in NFL history, which the Giants lost 23–17.

### GOING TO GET GRANGE

In the second half of the 1925 season, Tim Mara, owner of the newly enfranchised New York Giants, was all too aware that he was doling out much more money than the Giants were bringing in. He thought he had to do something to get paying customers into the Polo Grounds, and he had an idea.

Mara told Harry March (the Giants' general manager) that he was going out to Illinois to sign up the most dazzling star ever to hit college football, Harold "Red" Grange. The great breakaway back, who could lure sixty to seventy thousand fans into college stadiums to see him run with a football, was about to play his last college game. Mara's plan was to sign him and get him in a Giants uniform to play against the Chicago Bears at the Polo Grounds. It would save the franchise, Mara told March, and then he promptly reserved a drawing room on the 20th Century Limited to Chicago. From there he would go to Champaign to meet with Grange.

**A picturesque moment, but where are the fans? Only a handful were there to watch Hugh "Bones" Taylor go up for a Sammy Baugh pass in a game against the Packers in Green Bay. Taylor had a fine career and otherwise played before a legion of Redskins fans during his eight-year career in Washington (1947–54); when he retired he held every team mark for pass catching.**

**A strange sight to behold: legendary Giants linebacker Lawrence Taylor (No. 56) merely watching the action in this meeting with the Redskins, which was for the NFC title in 1986 (the Giants won 17–0). Normally Taylor, who played his college ball at North Carolina, was *the* center of action, as every opposing quarterback and running back could painfully attest.**

Wellington Mara, Tim's son, remembered that everyone was very excited about the prospect, and after a few days, the family received a telegram:

**Partially successful STOP Returning on train tomorrow STOP Will explain STOP
Tim Mara**

"We couldn't figure out what 'partially successful' meant," Wellington later explained. They found out on his father's return. "He'll be playing in the Giants-Bears game here," the elder Mara told them. "Only he'll be playing for the Bears."

George Halas and Dutch Sternaman, co-owners of the Chicago Bears, had been dealing with Grange's manager, C. C. Pyle, earlier and had struck an incredible deal to get Grange. Pyle would arrange two postseason tours of the United States, 17 games in all, and it would take the Bears from New York to Florida to California, with Grange and Pyle splitting profits 50–50 with the Bears. It was a deal that would bring Grange and Pyle approximately $250,000 in gate receipts alone and one that was impossible for Mara to compete with. Still, Tim Mara had been "partially successful" in getting Red Grange to play at the Polo Grounds in 1925.

The ever-controversial Duane Thomas has a few unpleasant words with a fan during the 1973 preseason. He was wearing a Washington Redskins uniform that day, his career with the Cowboys having ended after the 1971 season when he was traded to the San Diego Chargers. After sitting out the 1972 season, Thomas joined the Redskins in 1973 and played for two years before his stormy four-year NFL career came to a close.

## THE DRAFT

In Dallas, Gil Brandt, as director of player personnel, worked for Tex Schramm and proved himself to be one of the most astute observers of football talent ever in the National Football League. While the Cowboys were considered to be "America's Team," he was busy filling the roster with one outstanding player after the other. Draft day was his moment. This is what he had to say about it.

"It's like a beauty contest. It's easy to pick out the top one, two, or three girls, but then the rest of them look the same."

## SUMMERALL'S MOMENT IN THE SNOW

Many unpredictable things have happened on a professional football field, but not many were less likely than Pat Summerall's miraculous 49-yard field goal in a dizzying snowstorm in 1958 to defeat the Cleveland Browns and clinch a tie for the NFL East crown. Gerald Eskenazi described the astonishing deed in his book *There Were Giants in Those Days:*

> "I couldn't believe Jim Lee [Howell, coach] was asking me to do that," says Summerall. "That was the longest attempt I'd ever made for the Giants. It was on a bad field, and it was so unrealistic. Most of the fellows on the bench couldn't believe it either."
>
> Meanwhile, Wellington Mara was up in the press box in the upper stand. . . . [and said,] "That Summerall kick was the most vivid play I remember. I was sitting next to Ken Kavanaugh and Walt Yowarsky and we all said, 'He can't kick it that far. What are we doing?'"
>
> It is credited as a 50-yard [actually 49-yard] attempt but, according to Summerall, "No one knows how far it had to go. You couldn't see the yard markers. The snow had obliterated them. But it was more than 50 yards, I'll tell you that. . . .
>
> "I knew as soon as I touched it that it was going to be far enough. My only thought was that sometimes you hit a ball too close to the center and it behaves like a knuckleball, breaking from side to side. It was weaving out. But when it got to the 10, I could see it was breaking back to the inside."
>
> In the locker room after the game, Tim Mara was as happy as his sons Jack and Wellington, coach Jim Lee Howell, and Summerall, all rolled into one. "What a kick," he said. "What a kicker. But what the hell, that's what I pay him for, and I'm glad to see he earned his money today."

**COWBOY INSIGHTS?**

The most famous, or infamous, press conference ever held involving the Cowboys was the one called by running back Duane Thomas in July 1971. Discontented with his contract and the way he thought he was being treated, he went to Dallas and set up his own press conference while the team was out in Thousand Oaks, California. At it, he called coach Tom Landry "a plastic man, no man at all"; player personnel director Gil Brandt "a liar"; and general manager Tex Schramm "sick, demented, and completely dishonest." When told of Thomas' description of him, Schramm shrugged, then laughed. "That's not bad," he said. "He got two out of three."

A legend on a sideline in the rain: Vince Lombardi weathers the storm here in Washington in 1969, his last year of coaching. Perhaps the most revered coach in NFL history, Lombardi, a member of Fordham's "Seven Blocks of Granite" in his college playing days, served as offensive coordinator for the New York Giants (1954–58) before taking over the head coaching duties in Green Bay. With the Packers he forged his legend: in nine seasons he compiled a record of 98–30–4, won five NFL titles, and coached the Pack to victories in Super Bowls I and II. He entered the Pro Football Hall of Fame in 1971, the year after his death. Redskins No. 70 is fellow Hall of Famer linebacker Sam Huff; No. 29 is defensive back Ted Vactor.

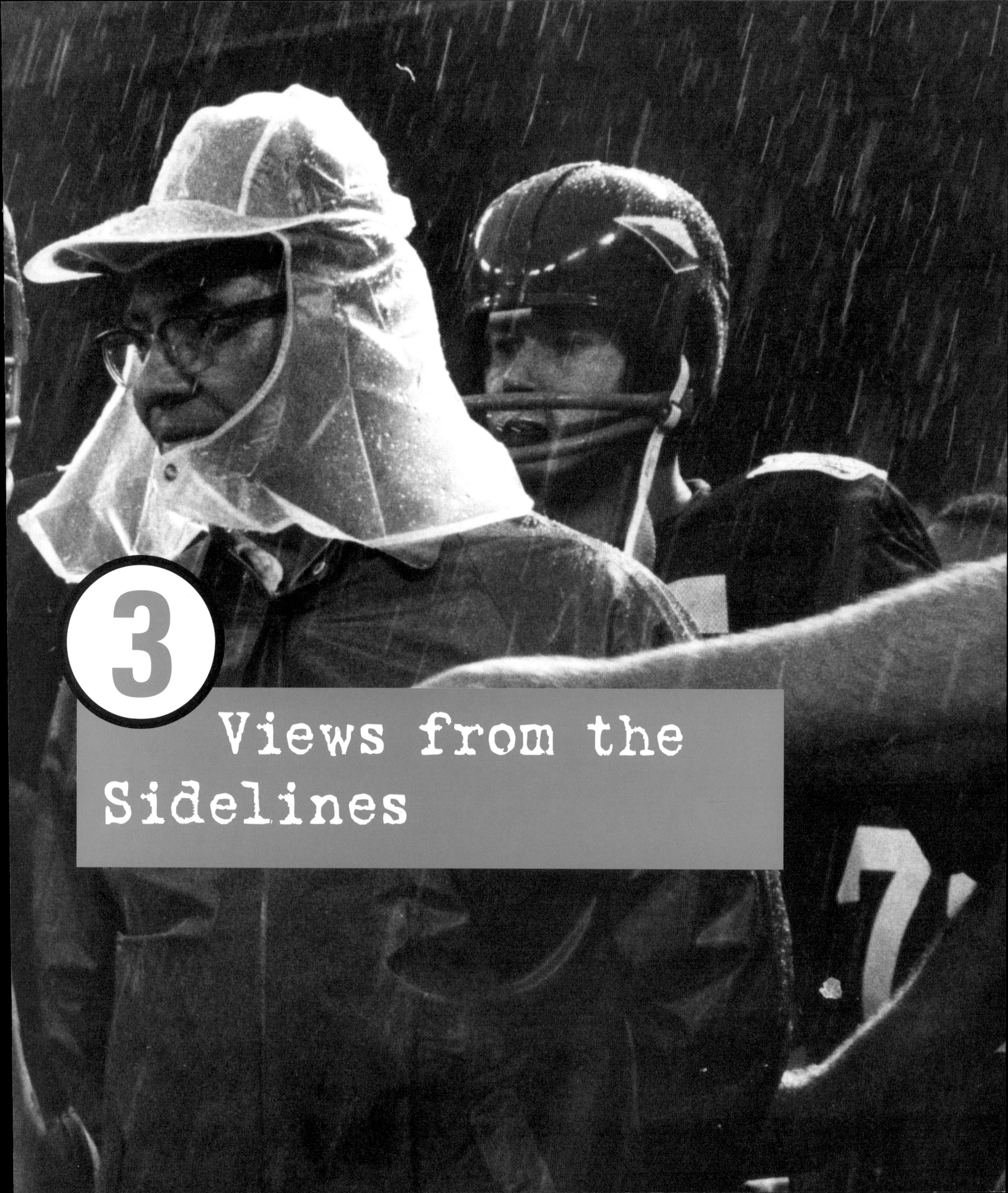

**3**

Views from the Sidelines

"If you're a pro coach, NFL stands for 'Not For Long.'"

—JERRY GLANVILLE

**A**mos Alonzo Stagg, the "Grand Old Man of College Football," who coached for 57 years at three different universities and finally retired at age 84, once said of the job, "To me, the coaching profession is one of the noblest and most far-reaching in building manhood." That may have been true back around the turn of the 20th century, but by the turn of the 21st century, in both college and professional football, the noblest and most far-reaching goal of a head coach is to produce a winner. Building character in the young men who play the game is still a part of it: the great self-discipline that must be instilled and maintained, the Herculean efforts that are demanded and must be expended, the intricate teamwork that is woven into a game plan, the spirit that must constantly be fueled and ignited. But, bottom line, pragmatism prevails; a coach needs to win if he wants a long career in the National Football League.

Professional football has been advanced and refined by a gilded roster of men who have taken on the overwhelming duties of head coach. The Chicago Bears' George Halas began coaching the year the NFL was launched, 1920, and guided his Monsters of the Midway through 40 seasons, still the longest tenure in league history. His 324 victories in regular-season and postseason play was the most until Don Shula (Colts and Dolphins) surpassed him in the nineties.

Besides Halas and Shula, there have been a number of other coaches in the NFL who merit the title *legend*. From the earlier days, Curly Lambeau led the Green Bay Packers and later the Chicago Cardinals and the Washington Redskins to 229 wins and six NFL championships in his 35 years at the helm; Steve Owen's New York Giants triumphed 151 times and won two NFL and eight division titles during his 22-year coaching career.

Earl "Greasy" Neale turned the perennial-patsy Philadelphia Eagles into a great team in the forties, with back-to-back NFL championships in 1948 and 1949. Paul Brown took over the Cleveland Browns in 1946 when the team was in the upstart All-America Football Conference; after they joined the NFL, he led them to five straight championship games—overall his teams took three NFL crowns and six divisional titles.

Weeb Ewbank won championships in both the NFL and the AFL during the years he piloted the Baltimore Colts and the New York Jets into major contenders. Sid

COACH LOMBARDI AND THE GREEN BAY GRASS DRILL

Lombardi's win-
ning percentage
of .740 is the
NFL's highest,
and during his
nine seasons
with the Packers
he led them
to five NFL
championships.

Gillman left his mark on both sides as well, with a reputation as one of the most imaginative and versatile minds in history, coaching the Los Angeles Rams, Los Angeles Chargers, San Diego Chargers, and Houston Oilers.

Then, of course, there were the two assistant coaches for the New York Giants in the late fifties, offensive coordinator Vince Lombardi and defensive coordinator Tom Landry, who went on to make names for themselves in Green Bay and Dallas, respectively. Lombardi's winning percentage of .728 is the NFL's highest, and during his nine seasons with the Packers he led them to five NFL championships. Landry is the league's third winningest coach behind Shula and Halas: 270 victories, five Super Bowl appearances, and two NFL championships.

There are many more who garner the highest of praise: Buddy Parker of the (Chicago) Cardinals, Lions, and Steelers; the Redskins' George Allen; Bud Grant

Watching from the bench in his raccoon coat is Harold "Red" Grange, between two unidentified Chicago Bears, in 1925, the year he would turn pro. After donning a Bears uniform the Galloping Ghost would spend little time on the bench and a lot of time on the playing field: in the first 12 days of the first leg of their barnstorming tour, Grange and the Bears would play *eight* games in *eight* different cities. On the second leg, they would play nine games in five weeks and travel across the country from the Atlantic to the Pacific.

of the Vikings; Chuck Noll of the Steelers; John Madden of the Raiders; Hank Stram of the Chiefs and the Saints; Chuck Knox of the Rams, Bills, and Seahawks; the Redskins' Joe Gibbs; Marv Levy of the Bills; and the 49ers' Bill Walsh. And there are coaches out there today edging their way toward this illustrious list of NFL legends.

But the views from the sideline, or in the locker room, or at training camp, or among the meetings and confrontations between players and coaches are not always practical business, as we shall see in the following pages.

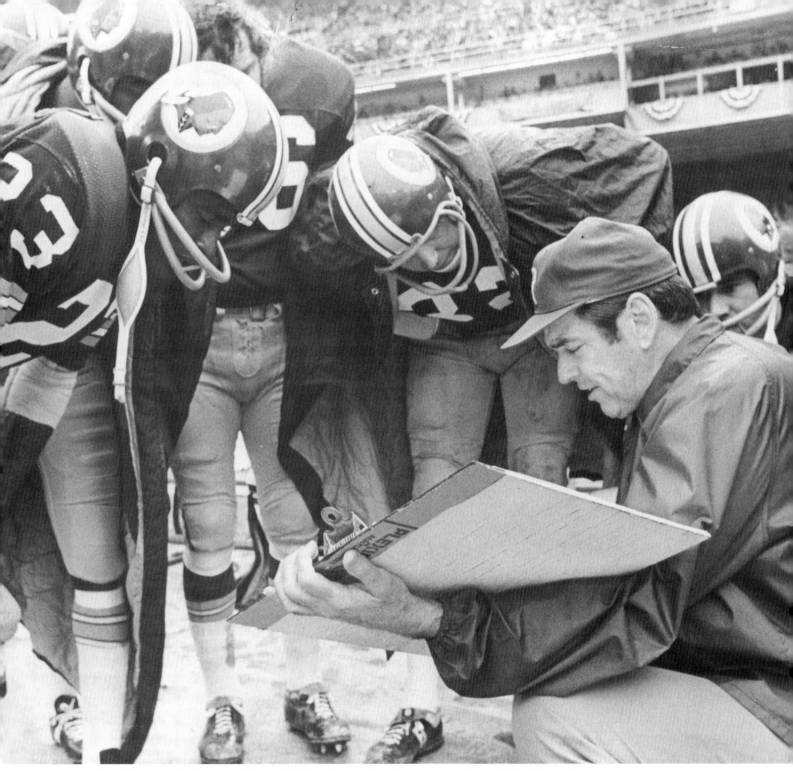

Redskins coach George Allen with his clipboard and some members of the "Over-the-Hill Gang" in 1972, the year he would take Washington to the Super Bowl (VII, where they would fall to the Miami Dolphins, 14–7). A defensive strategist of the first rank, Allen compiled a record of 67–30–1 during his seven years as head coach of the Skins and took his team to the playoffs five times. Identifiable players are Brig Owens (No. 23) and Jack Pardee (No. 32).

Whether it's pain or sorrow is unclear, but Sammy Baugh is not a happy Redskin on this bench. The game is the 1943 championship match with the Chicago Bears. Baugh suffered a concussion in the first half but returned later in the game; the Redskins still lost 41–21. A native of Sweetwater, Texas, Baugh was rarely seen on the Washington bench because when he wasn't quarterbacking, he was playing defensive back or punting the football.

## HALAS AND A CREATIVE REFEREE

The legendary halfback Red Grange remembered that refereeing was a little looser in the twenties and early thirties than it is today—open, so to speak, to improvisation. He liked to tell these stories about his coach's encounters with a rather creative referee:

> They had a referee in the twenties, Jim Durfee, who was a character. He and [Chicago Bears head coach] George Halas were pretty good friends. But Durfee loved to penalize the Bears right in front of the bench. When Halas was riding him pretty hard in a game one day, Jim began marching off a 5-yard penalty. Halas got really hot. "What's that for?" he hollered.
>
> "Coaching from the sidelines," Jim yelled back. (It was in fact illegal in those days.)
>
> "Well," said George, "that just proves how dumb you are. That's 15 yards, not 5 yards!"
>
> "Yeah," said Jim, "but the penalty for your kind of coaching is only 5 yards.'"
>
> Another day Jim was penalizing the Bears 15 yards and Halas cupped his hands and yelled, "You stink!" Jim just marched off another 15 yards, then turned and shouted, "How do I smell from here?"
>
> After the game, however, they'd probably have a drink together.

William "Lone Star" Dietz coached the Redskins in 1933 and 1934, posting a record of 11–11–2, and was notorious for using trick plays, sometimes to the consternation of his own team. Before coming to Washington, he coached on the college level at Washington State, Purdue, Louisiana Tech, Wyoming, Haskell, and Albright.

## LOMBARDI'S COACHING CREDO

The great Green Bay Packers coach summed it up in one brief sentence:

> If you *aren't* fired with enthusiasm, you'll *be* fired with enthusiasm.

## THE VIEW FROM THE TOP

George Preston Marshall, owner of the Redskins, often told this story of Will "Lone Star" Dietz, who was coach when the team was still in Boston. The Redskins were hosting the New York Giants one Sunday:

Things appear a bit on the grim side on this Washington bench in 1948. So say the expressions of Bones Taylor (left), Joe Tereshinski (center), and John Hollar (right). But they were smiling later: the Redskins beat the Detroit Lions that day, 46–21.

New York Giants head coach Allie Sherman holds court on the sideline with quarterback Y. A. Tittle and backfield coach Kyle Rote (also a star flanker for New York from 1951 to 1961) in 1963. Sherman took the Giants to the NFL title game that year, but there they fell to the Bears, 14–10. In his nine years at the helm (1961–68), Sherman compiled a record of 57–51–4.

A pair of Packers greats during a moment of rest on the sideline: offensive linemen Forrest Gregg (left) and Jerry Kramer. Gregg, out of Southern Methodist University, played 14 years for Green Bay and 1 with the Dallas Cowboys and earned a berth in the Pro Football Hall of Fame, inducted in 1977. Kramer, who played college ball at Idaho, was a mainstay from 1958 through 1968 and is best remembered for having thrown the key block in the 1967 Ice Bowl for Bart Starr's game-winning, quarterback-sneak touchdown and for later authoring the best-selling football book *Instant Replay*.

Who says they're stone-faced? Tom Landry and Bud Grant are all smiles here. And they have plenty to smile about— they're regarded as two of the finest coaches in the history of the game. Landry, the Dallas Cowboys' first coach, led the team from 1960 through the 1988 season, an overall record of 270–178–6, including two NFL champi-onships. Grant guided Minnesota from 1967 through 1983 and then again in 1985, produc-ing an overall record of 168–108–5 and taking the Vikings to the play-offs 12 times, including four Super Bowl appearances.

Dietz had heard that Lambeau and Halas had a coach high up in the stands who radioed instructions down to the bench. He thought it was a good idea, so good that he decided *he* would direct the Redskins from the upper deck of the stadium where we played. He had this walkie-talkie-like thing that he could use to talk to another coach on the bench.

This was the first time he planned to use it. And he had another strategy that day as well. On the sideline just before the game he instructed the team to kick off, no matter whether they won the toss or not. His plan was to get the Giants deep in their territory and hold them there. Then he trotted into the stands and back to the ramp that led to the upper deck. When he finally got to his station, he looked down on the field and saw the Redskins lined up to receive the football. He grabbed the walkie-talkie and shouted into it to his coach down below, "What the hell's going on? I said to kick the ball. Not receive. What the hell are we doing receiving it?"

There was a pause, then his assistant coach said, "We did kick. Harry Newman ran it back 94 yards for a touchdown."

## SHULA KNOWS THE WAY

Don Shula was the first coach to take more than one team to the Super Bowl. He led the Colts in Super Bowl III and the Dolphins in Super Bowls VI, VII,

Two Chicago stalwarts of the Bears' awesome defense of 1985, the team that went to Super Bowl XX and prevailed: tackle William "Refrigerator" Perry (left) and linebacker Otis Wilson. Perry, an anomaly at 300-plus pounds in the mid-eighties, came to the Bears from Clemson and played nine seasons; Wilson, from Louisville, played eight years in Chicago during that decade.

VIII, XVII, and XIX. His six appearances (two wins, four losses) are a record for a head coach. He also is the only coach to lead a team into the Super Bowl in the sixties, seventies, and eighties.

### ROONEY ON NOLL

Art Rooney, owner of the Steelers and also a racetrack owner, explained why he selected Chuck Noll as head coach: "His pedigree is super. He was by Paul Brown, out of Sid Gillman, by Don Shula."

### STOUT STEVE

Steve Owen was the head coach of the New York Giants from 1931 through 1953, and he played tackle for them for five years before that. He was a well-known sports figure in New York City, and dean of sportswriters Grantland Rice wanted to immortalize him in verse with this paean he penned in the forties:

> **"Stout Steve" is the name you've got—**
> **the moniker that you've earned—**
> **Stout in body and stout in heart,**
> **wherever the tide has turned,**
> **One of the best who has come along**
> **in this morbid vale of tears,**
> **A massive fellow who rides the storm**
> **in the march of passing years.**
> **Never a boast and never a brag**
> **and never an alibi,**
> **But the breed we label in any sport**
> **as a typical four-square guy,**
> **A mighty hunk of the human mold,**
> **blown from the rugged West,**
> **Whatever the odds from the off-side gods—**
> **A fellow who gives his best.**

Sideline communications: Washington's colorful quarterback Sonny Jurgensen talks to a coach upstairs. After seven seasons with the Philadelphia Eagles (1957–63), he was traded to the Redskins, where he played out the last 11 years of his heralded NFL career (1964–74). Considered by many the best pure passer the game has ever seen, Jurgensen was elected to the Pro Football Hall of Fame in 1983.

### DITKA'S JOB OF A LIFETIME

Mike Ditka, the first great tight end in professional football, played for the Chicago Bears initially and had many run-ins with "Papa Bear" George Halas. The result was that Ditka was eventually traded away and finished his NFL career in Philadelphia and Dallas. Halas, however, had great respect for Ditka, feeling he embodied everything that he admired in a football player.

Ditka had a special affinity for the Bears as well, and a liking for the grand old man of the game. In 1982, Halas summoned Ditka back, this time hiring him as head coach. Ditka remembers it this way:

> **At the time all the fair-haired guys were coming in, the new geniuses of football. I think Mr. Halas was trying to check me out [during an interview for the job] to see if I was one**

**Pittsburgh coach Chuck Noll, on the sideline here with his most productive quarterback, Terry Bradshaw, guided the Steelers for 23 years (1969–91), winning 209 games overall while losing 156 and tying 1. His teams won four championships in the seventies (Super Bowls IX, X, XIII, and XIV). Noll became a member of the Pro Football Hall of Fame in 1993. Bradshaw preceded him to the hallowed Hall, entering it in 1989.**

Happiness on the Redskins sideline, evinced by the smiles of two of the team's great wide receivers of the eighties and early nineties, Ricky Sanders (No. 83) and Gary Clark (No. 84). The year was 1987 and smiles were appropriate because the Skins went on to triumph in Super Bowl XXII. Sanders caught two touchdown passes in that game and Clark another as Washington trounced the Denver Broncos 42–10. Seen between the two is defensive end Charles Mann (No. 71).

of them, and so he asked me what my philosophy of football was. I kind of laughed, and I said, "You know, I don't think that's important. First of all, my philosophy is the same as yours, and that's strictly to win. How we do it—we have our methods and we have our ideas, but if you're asking me am I going to go out and throw the ball all over the ballpark like it's a wounded duck, no, I'm going to play football and teach good, basic fundamentals...." Then he offered me a two-year contract.

Ditka turned it down, saying he had to have at least three years. Halas gave it to him. Three years later the Bears won Super Bowl XX.

### HINKY-DINKY

Said Vince Lombardi in 1967:

> There is no room for second place here.
> There's only one place here, and that's first place. I've finished second twice in my time here, and I don't ever want to finish second again. There's a second-place bowl game, and it's a hinky-dinky football game, held in a hinky-dinky town, played by hinky-dinky football players. That's all second place is: hinky-dinky.

### TO KNEEL OR NOT TO KNEEL

Billy Kilmer told this story from the days when he was quarterbacking the New Orleans Saints:

> It was in 1970, a few weeks before [head coach] Tom Fears was fired. Things were coming apart. But big [Hall of Fame defensive end] Doug Atkins was doing a slow burn because he didn't want Fears to lose his job. Anyway, it was a game at Tulane Stadium and we were lined up for the kickoff.
>     Richard Neal was a second-year player for the Saints that year and Fears had him on the special teams. Fears apparently wanted to be sure Neal knew he was supposed to go down on the kickoff rather than play it soft.

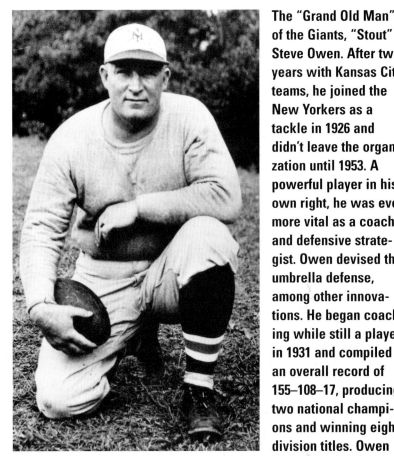

The "Grand Old Man" of the Giants, "Stout" Steve Owen. After two years with Kansas City teams, he joined the New Yorkers as a tackle in 1926 and didn't leave the organization until 1953. A powerful player in his own right, he was even more vital as a coach and defensive strategist. Owen devised the umbrella defense, among other innovations. He began coaching while still a player in 1931 and compiled an overall record of 155–108–17, producing two national champions and winning eight division titles. Owen was enshrined in the Pro Football Hall of Fame in 1964.

"There is no room for second place here. There's only one place here, and that's first place."

—VINCE LOMBARDI

A touch of sideline tenderness: Giants linebacker Lawrence Taylor gives a little hug to assistant coach Lamar Leachman. The hugs the great Taylor gave on the field of play were not so gentle, contributing to his reputation as one of the greatest—if not *the* greatest—outside linebackers in NFL history. For 13 seasons (1981–93), Taylor lit up the Giants defense; he was All-Pro nine times and went to 10 Pro Bowls. "L.T.," as he was best known, was inducted into the Pro Football Hall of Fame in 1999.

George Halas

**Chicago Bears coaches George Halas (1920–29, 1933–42, 1946–55, 1958–67) and Mike Ditka (1982–92) are captured in caricature by artist Bob Kilcullen. What is unique here is that Kilcullen played for Halas and with Ditka (when Ditka was a tight end) during his pro football career in Chicago (1957–66). A defensive end and tackle out of Texas Tech, Kilcullen was part of the Bears' 1963 championship team; then he went on to pursue a career in art, his work appearing in exhibitions in New York, Chicago, and Dallas among other venues.**

On the sideline, Chicago Bears coach George Halas goes over the playbook with rookie quarterback Bobby Layne in 1948. On the bench in the background, the faces of three Bears Hall of Famers can be seen: George Connor (left), Bulldog Turner (between Halas and Layne), and Sid Luckman (right).

So Coach Fears cups his hands and yells, "Neal down, Neal down."

Nobody could figure out what he was saying. The guys on the field kept looking trying to make it out and the same thing with guys on the bench. All of a sudden this booming voice comes roaring down the sidelines. It's Atkins bellowing, "Dammit, you heard the coach. Kneel down. Kneel down!"

Well, everybody on the team hit the ground in a kneeling position. Fears threw his hands up in disgust. He screamed, "No . . . Neal down." Atkins misunderstood again and boomed, "Kneel down, you bums." By this time, some of the rookies were literally digging themselves into the turf. It was crazy.

## LEGENDARY LANDRY

Tom Landry was a fine defensive back for the New York Giants, but he is best remembered as the great coach of the Dallas Cowboys during their heyday of the seventies and eighties. He was equally renowned for his countenance, a smile never crossing his face while he strode the sideline, not even a trace of any identifiable emotion. It prompted this observation from comedian Don Rickles:

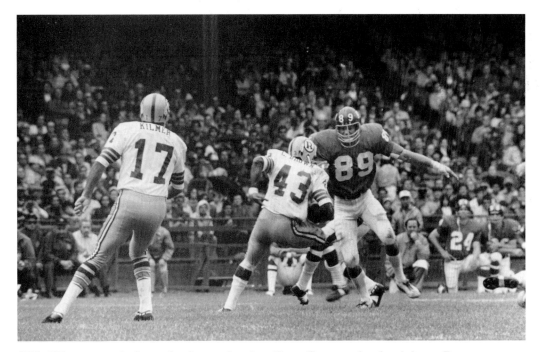

Billy Kilmer, caught in action here after handing off to running back Larry Brown, was one of the Redskins' most dependable (and colorful) quarterbacks. Coach George Allen brought Kilmer to Washington in 1971 as a charter member of the "Over-the-Hill Gang." At 31, the UCLA alum had already spent four years with the San Francisco 49ers and another four with the New Orleans Saints before coming to the nation's capital. He had another eight seasons in him before retiring after the 1978 season.

There's seventy thousand people going bananas, and there's Tom Landry on the side-line trying to keep his hat on straight. Once he got into a grinning contest with Mount Rushmore, and Mount Rushmore won.

### OOPS

Vince Lombardi was so emotional during the actual playing of a game that he often bore little resemblance to the man who so painstakingly managed every detail before the whistle blew.

Once, when he was the Fordham freshman coach in a game against Rutgers, Vince didn't like what he saw on the offensive line and began screaming for a substitute guard.

Three plays later the coach was still dissatisfied.

"I wanted that new guard in there," he snapped at an assistant coach.

"I know."

"Well, did you send him in?"

Tom Fears, a 60-minute end, chasing down Bears great Sid Luckman. Fears had a Hall of Fame career with the Los Angeles Rams (1948–56; inducted in 1970). A product of UCLA, Fears was the end at the other end of the offensive line from Elroy Hirsch and a favorite target of Hall of Fame passers Bob Waterfield and Norm Van Brocklin. He was also a fierce defensive player. Fears had a less successful NFL coaching career, three years leading the New Orleans Saints (1967–70; record: 13–34–2).

John Madden, striding the sideline here, coached the Oakland Raiders from 1969 through 1978, compiling a record of 112–39–7. His win percentage of .731 is one of the best in NFL history. In his 10 years as head coach, he led the Raiders to the playoffs eight times and won the league title in 1976 when Oakland defeated the Minnesota Vikings, 32–14, in Super Bowl XI. After leaving the coaching ranks, Madden went on to a long and distinguished career as a television football analyst.

"No."

"Dammit, what do you think this is? Why the hell didn't you tell him to get off the bench and get in there and plug that hole?"

"I couldn't."

"You better have a damn good reason, mister!"

"I do. He's already in the game."

## TRICK PLAYS

Lone Star Dietz was a colorful coach in many ways, from his Indian outfits to his trick plays—which, incidentally, never worked. Cliff Battles described the plays in an interview with Bob Curran, for his book *Pro Football's Rag Days*:

> He had a fondness for trick plays. One of these was the Fake Fumble. On the Fake Fumble play the tailback would get the pass from center and then fake a fumble. At this the defense was supposed to relax. Then the tailback would either leap into the air and throw a pass or he would run with the ball.

**Intensity personified: New York Giants head coach Bill Parcells bristles over the shoulder of an NFL official during a game. Fiery, outspoken, intimidating—a lot of adjectives have been used to describe Parcells, who led the Giants from 1983 to 1990; during that era Parcells built a record of 85–52–1, taking the Giants to Super Bowl XXI where they demolished the Denver Broncos, 39–20, and Super Bowl XXV to edge out the Buffalo Bills, 20–19. Parcells returned to coaching in 1993 with the New England Patriots; after four years there he moved to the New York Jets for three more, retiring after the 1999 season. In 2003 he was wooed back to take command of the Dallas Cowboys.**

Then there was the Broken Shoelace play. One of our players would pretend he had broken a shoelace and we would all pretend we had taken a timeout. When the defense relaxed, we would do almost anything.

We didn't like these plays. I didn't especially because I always ended up getting pounded harder than usual by the other team. Lone Star used to take our quarterbacks aside and bribe them. He'd give them money out of his own pocket if they would call these special trick plays.

When I found out about the bribes, I told him that he was going to give me special compensation for the pounding I took on those plays. Nothing came of that, of course.

## PEP TALK

Several decades after the 1943 playoff game between the Redskins and Giants to determine the NFL East title, Dutch Bergman explained to *Washington Evening Star* columnist Lewis F. Atchison how he tried to spur the Skins after they had lost two consecutive games to the Giants on the two preceding Sundays. Atchison duly reported it in his column in 1964:

> It was a cheerless, dispirited group when Bergman entered the room for his pregame. A definite "let's get it over with" atmosphere was in the air and he sensed it.
>
> "I just want to say," he began in slow, precise words, "that we have some good ballplayers on this squad and we have some yellow-bellied, gutless ones too. I know that some of you already have bought train tickets and are leaving for home right after the game. You're going out there, take your beating, and slink home like whipped dogs. You don't want to play the Giants. You're yellow, gutless. . . ."
>
> "Wait a minute there, you can't call me yellow," Sammy Baugh angrily broke in. "Nobody's gonna call me a quitter."
>
> The rangy quarterback took a couple of menacing steps forward, but Dutch held his ground.
>
> "All right, Sam, if you want to fight go out and fight the Giants," he calmly replied. "I'll be here in this room after the game. I'll be waiting for you."

It worked. The Redskins went out and scalped the Giants 28–0, and Baugh, with his passing, is credited with having led them to the victory.

**Johnny Blood McNally** is best remembered as a scatback runner and a fine pass receiver— and as one of the game's most colorful personalities. Blood, the name he adopted just before entering the pro game, played for five teams during his 14-year NFL career (1925–1938): the Milwaukee Badgers, Duluth Eskimos, Pottsville Maroons, Green Bay Packers, and Pittsburgh Pirates. The last three years, he was a player/head coach but produced a dismal 6–19–0 record. As a player, however, he earned his way into the Pro Football Hall of Fame, entering in 1963.

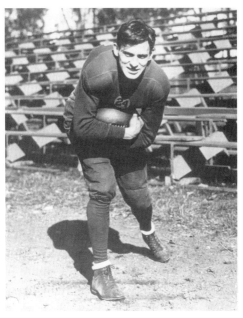

It ain't always fun and games. . . .

**And let us not forget the cheerleaders who grace the sideline, among them an early Dallas Cowboys troupe and a later Washington Redskins corps (with mascot).**

## SPIES

Was George Allen the perpetrator of clandestine deeds, the employer of surreptitious agents? Only Allen himself knows—or if he was, only Allen and his undercover army know—but many a rival NFL coach would swear that Allen and/or members of his coaching staff were prone to spying on the closed practice sessions of his upcoming opponents.

There was the time in Philadelphia, for example, when Eagles trainer Otho Davis swore that he saw a member of Allen's staff, dressed in dungarees and wearing a welder's hat, lurking about the otherwise empty stands of Veterans Stadium while the Eagles were preparing for the game against Allen's Washington team.

Another incident of similar repute occurred when Allen was guiding the Rams in 1967. It seems Tex Schramm, then Dallas Cowboys general manager, announced to the press that a suspicious-looking yellow Chevrolet had been parked across from the team's practice field. He had taken down the license number and after a little investigation had determined that it was a Hertz rental car that had been rented to, of all people, Johnny Sanders—then chief of the Rams' scouting system.

Allen immediately retorted with a countercharge. He said that his coaching staff had observed a man sitting up in a eucalyptus tree with binoculars, spying on the Rams' practice session. They had chased the man but had not caught him. According to Allen, however, the man looked an awful lot like Frank "Bucko" Kilroy, the former Philadelphia Eagles All-Pro guard who was now employed by the Cowboys as a scout.

If the two teams were spying on each other, Allen's secret service must have been more adroit, because the Rams annihilated the Cowboys the following Sunday, 35–13.

## COACH BLOOD

Johnny Blood McNally, the Hall of Fame halfback of the Packers and various other teams in the twenties and thirties, was also a player and head coach for the Pittsburgh Steelers from 1937 through 1939. Owner Art Rooney remembered it well:

> We once played a game in Los Angeles and John missed the train home. John was known to enjoy a good time, of course, so we didn't see him the whole week. On Sunday he stopped off in Chicago to see his old team, the Green Bay Packers, play the Bears. The newspaper guy asked him, "How come you're not with your team?" And John said, "Oh, we're not playing this week." Well no sooner did he get those words out of his mouth than the guy on the loudspeaker announced a score for the Philadelphia/Pittsburgh game. You couldn't depend on John a whole lot.

## TAKES ON LOMBARDI

Vince Lombardi's championship Packers revered their coach, but they also had some realistic and insightful opinions of the man.

From defensive tackle Henry Jordan: "He treats us all equally—like dogs."

From wide receiver Max McGee: "When he says, 'Sit down,' I don't even bother to look for a chair."

## AIN'T WORTH A DAMN

Bum Phillips, the Houston Oilers' outspoken coach of the seventies, had a view on just about every aspect of the game of football. Especially players.

"There's two kinds of players who ain't worth a damn," he said one day at the end of a press conference. "One that never does what he's told, and the other that does nothing except what he's told."

And, on another occasion, he offered this: "Every time you make a football player think, you're handicappin' him."

"Every time you make a football player think, you're handicappin' him."

—HOUSTON OILERS COACH
BUM PHILLIPS

Melee: when the Browns met the Redskins, opening day, 1966.

# 4

## Mayhem, Violence, and Pain

"We try to hurt everybody. We hit each other as hard as we can. This is a man's game."

—SAM HUFF, NEW YORK GIANTS, 1959

The game of football has always been a brutal one. Long before the pros decided to formalize their competition and launch a league of their own in 1920, there was worry about just how violent and dangerous the game of American football was. In 1906, President Theodore Roosevelt was so concerned about the sport and its "potential for injury or even death" that he summoned representatives from the major colleges playing the game in those days (among them Harvard, Yale, and Princeton) to the White House. There, he told them that if they did not reform the sport and regulate it, so that "its violence and brutality were tempered," he would see to it that the sport was banned in the United States.

Well, the sport *was* regulated on the college level and later among the pros, but it remained fiercely competitive, with bone-jarring collisions among super athletes, a vicious battleground where strength, speed, power, and ferocity were the virtues of the winners. And that is, in more than small part, where the enduring popularity of the sport comes from.

Jim Thorpe was the first true legend of the game, and it was his awesome power on the field for which he was remembered by all those who played against him. The Sac and Fox Indian, who put tiny Carlisle Institute on the football map, left bumps, bruises, and scars on opposing players when he played for such pro teams as the Canton Bulldogs, the Oorang Indians, and other teams of the early NFL. With his blend of power and speed, he defined the essence of the game of professional football.

Many greats followed in his footsteps, striking fear and frustration in their enemies' hearts. Over the years there have been the great individual confrontations where opposing players have waged special war upon each other: the Bears' Bronko Nagurski and the Packers' Clarke Hinkle, the Giants' Sam Huff and Green Bay's Jim Taylor, the Steelers' Jack Lambert and just about anybody across the line of scrimmage from him.

In the earlier days, players went both ways— 60-minute men, they were called. People sometimes forget that such dazzling runners as Red Grange and Johnny Blood McNally and quarterbacks like Sammy Baugh and Sid Luckman got the chance in every game to get in their own licks because they were also the best defensive backs

**Giants linebacker Sam Huff, a portrait in grit and grime. Huff, from West Virginia, was drafted by New York in 1956; he stayed around as an All-Pro middle linebacker through the 1963 season, an era in which the Giants won a league title (1956) and six divisional championships. Traded to the Redskins in 1964, he played five years there. Huff was elected to the Pro Football Hall of Fame in 1982.**

Things are not always right side up, as Chicago Bears tight end Greg Latta illustrates in this encounter with a Philadelphia Eagle.

in the game. The Eagles' Chuck Bednarik was an All-Pro as a center on offense *and* a linebacker on defense, the Bears' George Connor as an offensive tackle *and* a linebacker; Bronko Nagurski was as savage a tackler as he was a powerful runner.

Synonymous with the term *mayhem* in pro football are names like Dick Butkus, Ray Nitschke, Gino Marchetti, Jim Brown, Walter Payton, Jack Tatum, Mean Joe Greene, and many, many more. Some gave it out tackling, others by the way they ran; all are known for the way they hit.

Today the players are much bigger. Where a lineman might have been 220 pounds in the twenties and thirties, 250 or 260 pounds in the sixties or seventies, today many send the scales beyond the 300-pound mark. All are fast; power is the defining quality.

Collisions on NFL fields of play are thunderous; mayhem fills the 60 minutes of playing time of each game; true pain is as much a part of playing the game as strategy is of coaching it. It takes a special breed indeed.

**There was no more feared runner in the thirties than fullback Bronko Nagurski of the Chicago Bears. In this photograph he offers a credible example of the pile-driving power he was known for. No. 26 is Bears center Milford Miller; No. 6 is Bears halfback Gene Ronzani. The Bronk is a member of the charter class of the Pro Football Hall of Fame (1963).**

"When you hit him at the ankles, it was like getting an electric shock. If you hit him above the ankles, you were likely to get killed."

—RED GRANGE ON BRONCO NAGURSKI

### ENCOUNTERING NAGURSKI

Red Grange on Bronko Nagurski:

When you hit him at the ankles, it was like getting an electric shock. If you hit him above the ankles, you were likely to get killed.

Mel Hein on Bronko Nagurski:

If you hit him low, he'd trample you to death. If you hit him high, he'd knock you down and run over you. The best way to tackle Bronko was to have your teammates hit him about the same time—one or two low, one or two high. He was the most powerful fullback that I ever played against in all my career. He had a big body and could get that body, that trunk, down and be able to throw his shoulder into you. If you didn't get under his shoulder, he just knocked you butt over teakettles.

**Crunch: Baltimore Colts linebacker Mike Curtis is drilled by New York Jets running back John Riggins. Riggins, out of Kansas, played for the Jets from 1971 through 1975 before going to Washington where he starred for the Redskins (1976–79, 1981–85). Curtis, who played college ball for Duke, had a fine career with the Colts (1965–75), then played a year with the Seattle Seahawks and two more with the Redskins.**

Steve Owen on Bronko Nagurski:

**He was the only man I ever saw who ran his own interference.**

Johnny Dell Isola on Bronko Nagurski:

**I had heard a lot about him, but I thought most of it was exaggerated. We were at the Polo Grounds when I first ran up against him. It was first and 10 and they gave the ball to Nagurski, up the middle. I put my head down and charged into the hole. We met at the line of scrimmage, and you could hear the thud all over the Polo Grounds. I had my arms around his legs and my shoulder dug into him. It was the hardest tackle I ever made, but I made it and said to myself, well, I guess that will show you, Nagurski! Then, as I was getting up, I heard the referee shout, "Second down and two!"**

## PLAYING HURT

Dallas Cowboys running back Walt Garrison offered this special memory of tight end Mike Ditka:

**Mike Ditka, who first defined the position of tight end in the NFL, gathers in a touchdown pass here for the Chicago Bears in a game against the Minnesota Vikings in 1962; the passer is Bill Wade (No. 9). Ditka had a Hall of Fame career as a tight end, playing for the Bears (1961–66), the Philadelphia Eagles (1967–68), and the Dallas Cowboys (1969–72). He later came back as head coach of the Bears (1982–92) and took them to triumph in Super Bowl XX. Still later he piloted the New Orleans Saints. Ditka was inducted into the Pro Football Hall of Fame in 1988.**

**The Green Bay Packers'
view of the Detroit Lions,
circa 1960.**

When Ditka joined the Cowboys [1969], defensive back Charlie Waters and Cliff Harris used to taunt [him]. "Ya, Mike, you got great moves." And they'd swivel their heads back and forth indicating the extent of Ditka's moves. . . .

Ditka would try his damnedest when he was running his routes to get those two little bastards up close enough so he could give them a forearm to the chops. Right before he made his cut, he'd try to cream our cornerbacks.

That was Ditka.

[He] got his teeth knocked out in an auto accident the year he joined us. He flipped his car up over on top of a parked car. Went through the windshield and broke his jaw. The dentist told Ditka, "We can wire your teeth shut but you can't play tomorrow. Or we can pull them."

Ditka said, "Pull the sonofabitches."

Well, as it turned out, they had to wire his jaw shut anyhow because it was broke. But he played all the same. You could hear him out on the field breathing through his teeth. "Hiss-haw, hiss-haw, hiss-haw." Sounded like a rabid hound. And you could hear that mad dog Ditka cussin' even with his mouth wired shut. "God da otherrucker."

### GREEN-LEG LANE

Former Chief, Cardinal, and Packer MacArthur Lane, on former Bears linebacker Dick Butkus: "One time he bit me. Another time he tried to break my ankle. Another time he tried to crack my leg. Nothing happened . . . I guess maybe my leg was too green."

### ROOMMATES

Otto Graham was the head coach of the Redskins when Joe Don Looney, the heralded running back from Oklahoma, arrived in Washington (after stints with the

If ever a picture captures a player doing what he did best, this one of Chicago Bears linebacker Dick Butkus (No. 51) crushing Packers back Dave Hampton would have to be at the top of the list. Butkus, from Illinois and a first-round Bears draft pick in 1965, took the game's oldest rivalry quite seriously and played with a ferocity that was legendary. He starred for the Bears through the 1973 season and became a member of the Pro Football Hall of Fame in 1979.

"One time he bit me. Another time he tried to break my ankle. Another time he tried to crack my leg."

—MACARTHUR LANE ON
DICK BUTKUS

Otto Graham, carrying the ball here in a game against the Los Angeles Rams, was one of the game's finest quarterbacks and the field leader of the great Cleveland teams of the late forties and early fifties. Coming from Northwestern University, he was converted from a single-wing tailback to a T-formation quarterback and played 10 years for the Browns (1946–55, the first four in the AAFC). When Cleveland joined the NFL in 1950, he led the team to six consecutive NFL title games, winning three of them. Later Graham was the head coach of the Washington Redskins (1966–68), where his record was less spectacular, 17–22–3. He was elected to the Pro Football Hall of Fame in 1965.

Giants, Colts, and Lions) with an NFL reputation of being someone who marched to a far different drummer than anyone else in the game.

Linebacker Sam Huff, who had been traded from the Giants, was asked to room with Looney. "They offered me a bonus if I would room with Joe Don to keep him out of trouble," Huff explained. "I said I would but it was one of the toughest things I ever did. I didn't trust him. I didn't know whether he was going to try to beat me up or what. I never slept much before a game."

The two did get into a fight. As Huff later described it:

> It was before the opening game in Philadelphia. We were out in full pads on a Friday
> . . . and it was hot and miserable. Looney is running the Philadelphia plays for our
> defense. They run a toss to the fullback, and Looney runs around the end. I go in pur-
> suit and kind of take it easy. Joe Don lowers his shoulder and runs over me. Then he

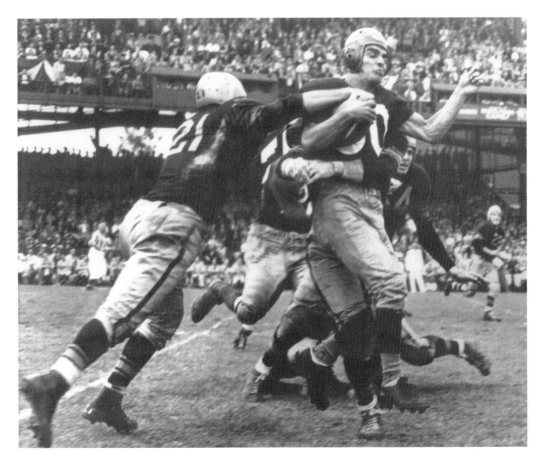

**Necktied and bear-hugged, Washington Redskins halfback Steve Bagarus is decidedly going no further with the football in this 1946 game with the Pittsburgh Steelers. Doing the necktie is Steelers linebacker Chuck Cherundolo.**

taunts me with the ball. Hell, this is just practice. I'm trying to save myself for the Philadelphia Eagles on Sunday.

I'm down on the ground, and he sticks the ball in my face and says, "How do you like that, big guy? I knocked the hell out of you."

I looked up at him and said, "You crazy so-and-so, you picked the right guy this time. You're gonna get yours."

The Washington Redskins' Glen "Turk" Edwards (No. 37), a behemoth in his time at 6'2" and 260 pounds, protects jump-passing quarterback Riley Smith here in a 1936 game. The following year, Edwards would be given the express duty of protecting Sammy Baugh, on whom owner George Preston Marshall was betting the Washington franchise. Playing both ways at tackle, Edwards was a dominating force in the scrimmage lines of the thirties. He returned to coach the Redskins from 1946 to 1948 but could only post a record of 16–18–1. The Turk was a good enough player, however, to merit inclusion in the Pro Football Hall of Fame, entering in 1969.

Brooklyn Dodgers ball carrier George Cafego is underwhelmed and overwhelmed on this play in a 1940 game against the Washington Redskins. Doing the underwhelming is center Bob Titchenal (No. 18), and doing the overwhelming is guard Steve Slivinski (No. 16). Hoping to join the whelming are end Wayne Millner (No. 40) and defensive backs Sammy Baugh (No. 33) and Jimmy Johnston (No. 31).

Chicago Bear George Connor delivers what looks like a knockout punch to the face of a Los Angeles Ram who tried to stop him after linebacker Connor intercepted a Rams pass in a game at the Los Angeles Coliseum. Connor, an All-American at Notre Dame, was one of the greatest 60-minute men the game ever produced, playing tackle on offense and either tackle or linebacker on defense. He joined the Bears in 1948 and remained through the 1955 season. He often earned All-Pro honors on *both* offense and defense, and he went to four Pro Bowls. He was elected to the Pro Football Hall of Fame in 1975.

So they came out of the huddle for the next play, and I know what the play is. Looney said to me, "All right, big guy, here I come again." I'm gritting my teeth. I'm going to nail this guy. When he got the ball, I came off the ground with my fist and hit him dead on the chin as hard as I could. He shook his head, his knees buckled, but he didn't go down. I gave him the best shot I could ever give him.

Then we got into a hell of a fight. They couldn't get us apart. [When it was finally over] Otto says, "I don't think you guys better room together this week."

## IN THE HEAT OF BATTLE

Protecting Sammy Baugh was the name of the game in the 1937 battle for the NFL championship. Coach Ray Flaherty reminded his team before the game that a healthy Baugh would be a major factor that day and it behooved all concerned to see that he stayed that way on the field of play.

The reminder was felt necessary because the George Halas–coached Chicago Bears, with certified monsters such as Bronko Nagurski, George Musso, and Joe

Another of the great 60-minute men, Clyde "Bulldog" Turner (No. 66) rambles with an interception here in a 1942 game against the Green Bay Packers. That year linebacker Turner, out of tiny Hardin-Simmons in Texas, set a Bears record with eight interceptions. An All-Pro center on offense and an All-Pro middle linebacker on defense, Turner played 13 seasons with the Bears (1940–52) and became a member of the Pro Football Hall of Fame in 1966.

**The great Jim Brown (No. 32) winces as a host of St. Louis Cardinals try to stop him. It ordinarily took several defenders to bring down this powerful and elusive Cleveland Browns running back, who many claim was the best all-around ball carrier the pro game has ever seen. When he retired after nine years in Cleveland (1957–65, during which time he never missed a single game), Brown had led the league in rushing in eight of them and gone to nine consecutive Pro Bowls. His enshrinement in the Pro Football Hall of Fame was in 1971.**

Stydahar, among others, had a deserved reputation of being tough, nasty, and downright dangerous.

Tackle Turk Edwards took it sincerely to heart and was heard more than once warning opposing defensive linemen that they had better not try any rough stuff with Slingin' Sam or horrendous retribution would be paid. In one overzealous moment, Edwards was so intent on protecting his passer that in his eagerness to block for Baugh, he backed over him, causing a 15-yard loss.

Later in the game, Chicago end Dick Plasman took special offense at something defensive back Baugh did on a pass play in which they had become entangled, and he threw a punch at Sammy. Unfortunately for Plasman, it was a short five yards from the Washington bench and, as Shirley Povich later described in the *Washington Post*, "Coach Flaherty was the first to leap to his feet and the first to rush to the battle scene. He tackled Plasman high—high around the mouth—with a set of knuckles and put an end to the battle."

CLEVELAND PLAIN DEALER

Baugh finished the game in good health, and the Redskins won.

### A PUNCH IN THE FACE

Hall of Fame tackle and linebacker George Connor, who played his entire NFL career with the Chicago Bears, liked to tell of his initiation into the game of professional football.

I got my initiation into the street-fighting arena that is more commonly known as the pro football line of scrimmage as a rookie in 1948. In the preseason I was used as a backup tackle for Fred Davis. He told me, "When I raise my hand coming out of the huddle, that means I need a rest. You come in on the next play."

I watched. When I saw his arm go up, I grabbed my helmet from the bench and, when the play was over, raced onto the field. As soon as the ball was snapped on the next play, my face ran smack into the fist of the lineman I was opposing. It was an especially unpleasant greeting in those days before face masks were routinely worn. I was startled but thought maybe this was the typical welcome a rookie got to the brutal game I'd heard that the pros played.

Later in the same game Davis raised his hand again, and I replaced him on the next play. This time I was lined up opposite a different lineman. But the reaction was the same. When play began, this lineman smashed me square in the face too.

After the game I tried to figure out why it was happening to me; perhaps they resented all the publicity I'd gotten as a rookie, or maybe it was because I came from Notre Dame—a lot of the pro players were less than fond of the Fighting Irish alumni in those days. I even asked a few other linemen about this so-called special greeting. They agreed that work in the line was violent as hell, but what was occurring to me did seem a little extraordinary.

It went on for several weeks. Then one Sunday it all became crystal clear. This time when Davis raised his hand, I for once kept my eyes on him rather than on

Cowboys quarterback Don Meredith, who took a beating himself in this 1967 game against the Redskins, consoles Washington quarterback Sonny Jurgensen at game's end. And what an end it was. With 1:10 left in the game, Jurgensen threw a touchdown pass to Charley Taylor to put the Skins ahead 14–10; Meredith led the Cowboys back in the final minute and tossed a touchdown pass to Dan Reeves to give Dallas a 17–14 victory.

"I got my initiation into the street-fighting arena that is more commonly known as the pro football line of scrimmage as a rookie in 1948."

—HALL OF FAME CHICAGO
BEAR GEORGE CONNOR

the play itself. When the ball was snapped, I saw Davis lunge across the line, punch the opposing player in the face, and then trot off toward our bench.

For the rest of the year I announced myself to whoever the opposing lineman was when I lined after coming into the game: "Connor in, Davis out!"

It made my life a lot easier that rookie year.

## DON'T SNEAK UP ON AN INDIAN

Joe Guyon, who played in the backfield with Jim Thorpe and under the legendary coach Pop Warner at Carlisle, and later in the NFL in the twenties with the Canton Bulldogs, Cleveland Indians, Oorang Indians, Rock Island Independents, Kansas City Cowboys, and New York Giants, remembered this incident in Chicago:

The games that were real scraps were the ones in Chicago. George Halas ran that team, and he was a scrapper. There'd be a fight every time we met those son of a biscuits. Halas knew that I was the key man. He knew that getting me out of there

**Mayhem at the Meadowlands: Giants running back Bob Hammond (No. 33) is brought down in a 1977 game against the Eagles while a lot of pushing and shoving goes on behind him (much of it among the Eagles themselves). In the foreground and on the ground is fullback Larry Csonka (No. 39), who played for New York from 1976 through 1978. Best remembered for his seven-year career with the Dolphins (1968–74) and his large contribution to the undefeated season of the 1972 Miami team, Csonka was inducted into the Pro Football Hall of Fame in 1987. The Giants were in their second season at the Meadowlands in New Jersey in 1977, after having played in New York City the previous 51 years. On top of Csonka is Giants guard Doug Van Horn.**

would make a difference. I was playing defense one time, and I saw him coming after me from a long ways off. I was always alert. But I pretended that I didn't see him. When he got close, I wheeled around and kicked him, goddamn. I brought my knee right up into him. Broke three of his ribs. As they carried him off, I said to him, "What the hell, Halas. Don't you know that you can't sneak up on an Indian?"

### IN THE TRENCHES

Bulldog Turner, one of the most ferocious 60-minute men of his time (center on offense, linebacker on defense), starred for the Chicago Bears throughout the forties and early fifties. He remembered the mayhem in an interview reprinted in Myron Cope's *The Game That Was*:

There was a guy named Tarzan White—oh, *goddamn!* He'd get so mad. And the madder he'd get, the blockeder he would get. I'd have him on his back before he could ever hit me. Goddamn, it was funny. Another guy I met was this big Ed Neal. There in the late forties he played at Green Bay, and by this time they had put in the 5–4

**A free-for-all in Chicago: the always-heated rivalry between the Chicago Bears and the Chicago Cardinals turns riotous in this 1956 game at Wrigley Field. To the left, Cardinals end and place-kicker Pat Summerall does battle with Bears wide receiver Harlon Hill (No. 87). To the right, Bears tackle Fred Williams (No. 75) leaps into another battle. The altercation was said to have resulted in a draw, but the Bears won the game, 10–3.**

In the muck and the mud, the Bears and the Lions illustrate that the game is neither a pretty nor antiseptic one. The ball carrier for the Bears in this game from the late sixties is Ralph Kurek.

defense, and they put the biggest, toughest guy they had right in front of the center. And I was expected to block him either way, according to which way the play went.

Well, this Ed Neal weighed 303 pounds stripped. His arms were as big as my leg and just as hard as that table. He could tell when I was going to center that ball, and he'd get right over it and hit me in the face. You didn't have a face guard then, and so that Ed Neal broke my nose seven times. Yes, that's right. No—he broke my nose *five* times. I got it broke seven times, but five times *he* broke it.

## BUTKUS AND BROWN

In his autobiography *Flesh and Blood*, Chicago Bears linebacker Dick Butkus recounted a precarious encounter with Cleveland Brown running back Jim Brown in the sixties. The two Hall of Famers escaped unscathed and went on to play another day.

There is one thing about that game that I will never forget. It happened late in the fourth quarter after the night had cooled down. We had put on a blitz. I shot the gap

Beheading, NFL style: New York Giants defensive back Merle Hapes (No. 44) appears to be trying to remove the head of Redskins running back Steve Juzwik in a 1942 game between the two longtime rivals, played in Washington. Juzwik's head stayed on, but the Skins lost that afternoon, 14–7.

between the left guard and tackle and there, standing between me and the quarterback, was Jim Brown, the man who, according to the sportswriters, never bothered to block. Well, he was waiting for me *that* night. When we made contact, we seemed to freeze for an instant before I started to make a move to get by him. Suddenly he had my left arm clamped under his left arm, and when he began to roll to his left, I realized that if I didn't get my arm out of that vise Jim had it in, he'd either hyperextend my elbow or break the arm altogether.

I slipped free just in time.

Why did he do it? I don't know. Maybe he didn't like the way I hit him earlier in the game. But deep down I think it was because he was Jim Brown. He was not going to let me get by him, even though it was just an All-Star game. Like all great athletes, Jim had a hidden reserve that he called upon in special moments.

## MIXING MAYHEM METAPHORS

The NFL title game of 1938 between the New York Giants and the Green Bay Packers, which the Giants won 23–17, was so exciting, so filled with mayhem, that International News Service reporter Arthur "Bugs" Baer just couldn't contain himself. His report:

It was a game of vibrating behemoths against fermenting Goliaths. Every man on the field was six feet tall, three feet wide and a yard thick. There was every kind of official on the turf except the one they needed most. And that was a knockdown timer.

When the two lines rushed at each other it was like a freight train kissing the depot. You could hear the crash from the rockbound shores of Maine to far prettier places. The score, 23–17, sounds like the little-potato-hard-to-peel had met the lumberyard skull busters who decided to mash them instead.

It was a backwoods vendetta in the high rent district. With the winners getting about $135 extra per man, it was this extra bit of muscular bribery that made the lads go to town like a wolf in famine.

The boys were as earnest as a sneak thief in a lock and key store. And as tough as veal breaded in marble dust.

"Bullet" Bill Dudley had a fine NFL career spread out over three teams. Coming out of Virginia, he joined the Pittsburgh Steelers in 1942 and returned to them after service in the war to play two more years before moving on to the Detroit Lions (1947–49) and finally to the Washington Redskins (1950–51, 1953). A fine ball carrier and an exceptional punt and kickoff returner, Dudley earned a place in the Pro Football Hall of Fame in 1966.

One of the most violent collisions ever on an NFL playing field occurred at Yankee Stadium in 1960, and it was between two Hall of Famers. In the first photo of this sequence, New York Giants flanker Frank Gifford (No. 16) hits the ground after a devastating collision with Philadelphia Eagles linebacker Chuck Bednarik (on the ground behind Gifford). In the second photo, Bednarik (No. 60) has risen, but Gifford remains on the ground unconscious. Gifford suffered a concussion that kept him out not only for the rest of that season but for 1961 as well. He made a fine comeback, however, in 1962 and played three more years for New York. Bednarik, one of the greatest 60-minute men in NFL history, played center on offense and linebacker on defense for 14 years (1949–62); he was inducted into the Pro Football Hall of Fame in 1967, a decade before Gifford was so honored.

**They went at each other like dogs meeting in a sausage machine. And mixed like the stuff they put in a Martini.**

**It was a throwback to the apes. Twenty-two muggs got an assist on the play and the apes got credit for the putout. . . .**

**It was mostly a barroom fight outdoors. Close to 50,000 innocent bystanders looked upon the resumption of gang warfare in America. It was terrific.**

## ON UNITAS

Pro Football Hall of Famer Art Donovan remembered his most famous teammate in Baltimore and a fellow Hall of Famer:

**No one ever saw John Unitas "sliding" into the grass after a scramble to avoid being tackled. Quarterbacks who did that were automatically labeled a sissy. Plus, when I first came into the league, you weren't ruled down until your forward progress was stopped. Today, it's when your knee touches the ground and an opposing player touches you. During the fifties, you used to see guys clawing for that extra yard with tacklers sitting on top of them trying to smash their skull. Running backs and quarterbacks naturally learned to give as good as they got.**

**Unitas dished out punishment when he ran. And he ran a lot. This business of not allowing your quarterback to run with the football is relatively new in the game. I realize it's because of all the money they pay these guys today. Owners want to protect their investment and all that. But I kind of agree with Steelers linebacker Jack Lambert, who said, "If they don't want 'em to get hit, why don't they just put a dress on 'em?"**

## IN A DAZE IN DALLAS

Cowboys wide receiver Buddy Dial remembered that everything wasn't always "Dandy" with quarterback Don Meredith:

**Against the Cards, he was hit so hard, he couldn't remember his teammates' names, and Landry left him in the game. Landry would send out the plays, but Danny Reeves had to interpret them for Meredith. I'm telling you, it's hard enough to play when your head is on straight, but when you get the crap knocked out of you, it's a little hard to remember who to give the ball to, never mind which team you're playing for.**

## MELEE

In one game against the Eagles, Los Angeles Rams linebacker Les Richter started roughing up Philadelphia quarterback Norm Van Brocklin, his former teammate. He started in the first quarter and kept up a running feud with the Dutchman throughout the game. Finally, when the game ended, Philadelphia linebacker Bob Pellegrini roared across the field, jumped Richter, and started fighting. Pellegrini then took a strong hold on the Rams' linebacker while several Eagles players got in some good licks. It could have developed into a brutal beating, but finally the police arrived and broke it up.

Richter's reaction to it all: "If you don't like to knock somebody down, you have no business in this game."

"If you don't like to knock somebody down, you have no business in this game."

—LOS ANGELES RAMS LINE-
BACKER LES RICHTER

## MYSTERIOUS WOUND

Dr. Bill Osmanski (a dentist after retiring from the game), the former Bears fullback, told this story about Pro Football Hall of Fame tackle Joe Stydahar:

> One day we [Chicago Bears] were playing Brooklyn, and Bruiser Kinard, the Dodgers' great tackle, was giving me a bad time. Once I was knocked out, and when Joe picked me up he asked who did it. I told him I wasn't sure. That it was either No. 52 or 25.
>
> Well, a couple of plays later, Stydahar and Kinard crashed together so hard that the force of the collision opened a deep gash in Kinard's arm and he had to go up to the clubhouse to have it stitched up. The officials believed just a collision couldn't cause such damage. They thought Joe must have been carrying a knife. In fact, they made a thorough search of all of us for concealed weapons. They even looked in Stydahar's mouth to see if he could have bitten Kinard. That was a waste of time if I ever saw one. Joe couldn't bite anybody. Not without teeth!

Stydahar took special pleasure in the fact that he had lost all his front teeth playing football.

## NOT-SO-NICE TIMES

Marion Motley and Bill Willis, both Pro Football Hall of Famers, were among the first African Americans to play in the National Football League, members of their race having been systematically excluded since the twenties. With the Cleveland Browns, first in the All-America Football Conference in 1946 and then in the NFL when the team joined that league in 1950, the two faced frequent unpleasantness because of the color of their skin. As Motley remembered:

> In the very beginning, [Browns coach Paul Brown] warned Willis and me. He said, "Now you know that you're going to be in many scrapes. People are going to be calling you names. They're going to be nasty. But you're going to have to stick it out."

It was rough, all right. If Willis and I had been anywhere near hotheads, it would have been another 10 years till black men got accepted in pro ball. We'd have set 'em back 10 years.

I still got many a cleat mark on the backs of my hands from when I would be getting up after a play and a guy would just walk over and step on my hand. . . . You can see the scars. I couldn't do anything about it. I'd want to kill those guys, but Paul had warned us. The referees would stand right there and see those men stepping on us, and they would turn their backs.

## KO BY AN SOB

Los Angeles Rams 60-minute man Tank Younger told of a memorable run-in with Chicago Bears owner and coach George Halas:

Well, we were playing in Chicago one day. I was at linebacker and Johnny Lujack went back to pass. He got hemmed up back there and started to run. This was right in front of Mr. Halas' bench, mind you. I moved in for the tackle and right then he jukes me. Now I'm out of position and he's about to run by. So I stuck out a hand and necktied him. He goes down, slams his head to the ground, and gets kayoed. Mr. Halas comes out on the field and yells at me: "Tank, you SOB, we're gonna kill you." Then he puts Sid Luckman in at quarterback, and the next three plays they come right at me. Stan West, the linebacker playing next to me, yelled over, "It's time to grab grass and growl." Somehow, I managed to weather the storm, and after the game, Halas runs out on the field and puts his arm around me. That's when he said, "Tank, you're the greatest, dirtiest, best football player in the league. I just wish we had you." And then he walked off.

> "Tank, you're the greatest, dirtiest, best football player in the league. I just wish we had you."
>
> —GEORGE HALAS TO LOS ANGELES RAM TANK YOUNGER

When asked later how this made him feel, Tank responded, "Very proud."

## THE BLOODIEST NOSE EVER

Steelers quarterback Terry Bradshaw told about a nosebleed he'll never forget . . . no matter how hard he tries:

Some of these injuries I remember more than others. The most painful injury I suffered in my career occurred at the end of a scramble during an exhibition game in Baltimore in 1978. Colts linebacker Stan White swung his arm around and accidentally shattered the cartilage in my nose. On the Bradshaw Pain Scale this rang the big bell. This was to pain what Johnny Unitas was to quarterbacks. Oh, my, did it

Tackle Joe Stydahar, 6'4" and 230 pounds, was known as one of the roughest, toughest linemen in the game in the late thirties and early forties. After college ball at West Virginia, he joined the Chicago Bears in 1936 and played through 1942; after wartime military service, he returned to Chicago in 1945 for two more seasons. With the Bears he was an All-Pro four straight years before going into the service, and he played in five NFL title games, three of which the Bears won. Later he was signed as head coach of the Los Angeles Rams (1950–51) and the Chicago Cardinals (1953–54); his overall coaching record is 22–29–1.

hurt. I never had anything hurt so badly in my life. My teammates didn't take it very seriously. They assumed it was just a bad nosebleed: "Hey, TB, talk to me when a couple of the bones are popping out of it." On the sidelines they put cold compresses on it to try and stop the bleeding. The bleeding won. At halftime they put me in the shower room, and when they went out to play the second half they left a security guard there to watch me. He watched me bleeding. "Boy," he said, very impressed, "that sure is a lot of blood you got there."

"Thank you," I mumbled. I lost so much blood I just about bled to death. Now that would have made a great headline: "Bradshaw Dies from Nosebleed." My friends would have been too embarrassed to attend my funeral.

A doctor finally got the bleeding stopped, and I flew home with the team. But when we reached a high altitude the pressure caused the bleeding to start again. Blood was just pouring out of my nose. When the plane landed, I was taken directly to the hospital and they operated the next morning. After the operation, newspapers reported: "Bradshaw Is Listed in Fair Condition." Fortunately, however, they did not finish that report, "with a bad nosebleed."

### WHERE AM I?

"Bullet" Bill Dudley, the Hall of Fame halfback who played for several NFL teams, is often reminded of this jolting encounter in the forties when he was playing for the Detroit Lions in a game against the Chicago Bears.

Dudley was having an exceptionally productive day, which provoked Bears lineman Fred Davis, whose grasp Dudley was eluding with regularity that afternoon—until one play near the end of the game. Davis got rid of his frustration with a thundering forearm to the side of Dudley's head.

Dudley went down in a heap and was helped off the field. On the bench, he just stared at his coach, Gus Dorais, and the team trainer who were standing before him, and then he finally asked, "Where am I?"

"In Chicago," the trainer told him.

"What's the score?"

"Fourteen to nothing, we're ahead," said Dorais.

"Am I married?"

"You are," Dorais said.

"Oh," Dudley said, and smiled.

## WELCOME TO THE NFL

Will Walls, an end out of Texas Christian University, made his NFL debut with the New York Giants in 1937. In the Giants' first preseason game with the Chicago Bears, a team with a reputation for being mean and ugly as well as extraordinarily good, Walls was introduced to the sometimes ungentle and ungentlemanly world of professional football.

On the first play after the kickoff, Walls found himself lined up across from Joe Stydahar: 6'4", 230 pounds, an All-Pro who was then working his way to a niche in the Hall of Fame. Stydahar, who often played without a helmet, was also known as one of the most rugged players in the league.

Walls admittedly was nervous. "I wasn't afraid of him, though," Walls said later, "more curious, I guess, to see if he was as tough as they said."

He was. As soon as the ball was snapped, Stydahar lunged across the line and slugged Walls, knocking him flat on his back.

Walls was stunned and furious and leaped to his feet. Stydahar looked at him dolefully. "Kid, I didn't mean to do that," he said. "Sometimes I just get too excited at the start of a game." He then patted Walls on the back and gave him a reassuring smile.

Walls said something to the effect that he could understand that and returned the smile.

On the next play, the reassured Walls was again face-to-face with Stydahar, and again Stydahar surged across the line at the snap like an enraged bull. This time it was a ferociously wielded forearm to the jaw that dulled Walls' senses and reintroduced him to the grass of the playing field.

The dazed rookie got up and found Stydahar looking at him and shaking his head. "You've got to stay alert, son," Stydahar said.

> "My joints hurt so much on Monday morning after a game that I would sometimes have to crawl from bed to the bathroom."
>
> —DICK BUTKUS

## BUTKUS ON PAIN

Pro Football Hall of Fame middle linebacker Dick Butkus, who played his entire NFL career for the Chicago Bears, is best known for *dispensing* pain: to running backs, quarterbacks, pass receivers, and anyone who tried to block him. He was not immune to pain himself, however, as he explained in his autobiography:

> I was able to push the pain down, lock it in until the game was over. I didn't know it then, but pain would be with me for the rest of my life. Toward the end of my career, my joints hurt so much on Monday morning after a game that I would sometimes have to crawl from bed to the bathroom.

A classic facemask infraction, only there weren't any face masks in 1948. That did not prevent Chicago Bears end Joe Abbey (No. 26) from grabbing for one. The unfortunate ball carrier being facemasked is Detroit Lions quarterback Fred Enke.

**5**

On the Wackier Side

"I don't have one bad memory from my 13 seasons; I don't have a memory at all, for that matter."

—BUBBA BAKER

**J**ust as major league baseball had its "clown prince," Al Schacht, and unique spokesmen, like Yogi Berra, professional football has had its own share of characters whose deeds on and off the field have entertained football fans of all eras. From Johnny McNally, who changed his name to "Blood" because he thought it would be a much more memorable "football name," to the rhyming boasts of Deion Sanders eight decades later, the National Football League has had some, well, unusual performers.

And in the more than 80 years that the NFL has been part of our lives, there have been incidents and events involving professional football players so unorthodox, so strange, so laughable that they deserve to be preserved for posterity along with all the sterling performances and unforgettable achievements resulting from more normal efforts.

There have been trick plays. Hall of Fame center Mel Hein collaborated with Giants quarterback Harry Newman on the shortest pass play in NFL history in the thirties. With some tricky shifting into a weird formation, he became an eligible receiver; after the snap, Newman just pushed the ball back into to Hein's hands and then whirled around as if he still had it. Hein lumbered down the field untouched for about 40 yards before anyone noticed he had the ball. Then there was Shipwreck Kelly, one of the most notorious roisterers off the field—on it, he could also be a tad different. A halfback playing for the Brooklyn Dodgers, a franchise Kelly had bought in the early thirties, he was back to receive a punt one Sunday afternoon; he caught the ball and as the opposing players swarmed toward him punted the ball straight back up the field.

Among the certifiable characters that succeeded Blood and Kelly, some have inscribed their memories in books that have entertained hundreds of thousands of football fans and just plain reading folk: the Cowboys' Pete Gent, Art Donovan of the Colts, the Lions' Alex Karras, Jerry Kramer of the Packers, the

Pete Gent: the irreverent, iconoclastic, and very funny Dallas Cowboy, who also just happened to be a pretty good football player when he was on the field of play. Gent, a wide receiver out of Michigan State, converted to flanker after joining the Cowboys in 1964; he played five seasons in Dallas. Afterward, he wrote a novel, *North Dallas Forty*, a ribald romp inside a mythical football team that surely resembled the Cowboys with characters that could easily be mistaken for Tom Landry, Don Meredith, and Tex Schramm; the novel was a national best-seller and was later made into a successful motion picture.

**Chicago Bears defensive back Don Kindt (No. 6) in action here in a 1950 game against the Los Angeles Rams. Bears tackle Fred Davis gets in a little mayhem of his own, delivering a right cross to the chin of Rams fullback Dick Hoerner. Kindt, from Wisconsin, played halfback on offense and defense for the Bears from 1947 through 1955.**

Bears' Dick Butkus, and the Steelers' Terry Bradshaw, among many others. On the other hand, Bubba Baker, defensive end for the Lions and the St. Louis Cardinals, spoke perhaps for the other end of the reminiscence spectrum when he said, "I don't have one bad memory from my 13 seasons; I don't have a memory at all, for that matter." Then there have been the brash and the outspoken, from Dallas' Duane Thomas to Chicago's Jim McMahon. And there's the legendary partying of Bobby Layne and Sonny Jurgensen . . . the antics of Doug Atkins and John Riggins . . . the comments and observations of Don Meredith and Mike Ditka.

For all the mayhem on the field of play, all the pain endured by those who play the game, and the anguish suffered by those who coach it, professional football still has its lighter side, its ventures into the bizarre, its own cultivated outrageousness. It is a sport whose players, and sometimes coaches, circumstances, and incidents, can bring a smile, a chuckle, even a guffaw to those involved as well as to the fans.

GENT STORIES

Pete Gent was a member of the Dallas Cowboys from 1964 through 1968, a flanker, wide receiver, and sometime tight end, who, during his tenure with the team, provided Dallas sportswriters with a cornucopia of anecdotes and laughs.

When his good friend Don Meredith was having his highs and lows at quarterback, having three passes intercepted one week by Ross Fichtner of the Browns and then throwing four touchdowns the next, Gent slapped him on the shoulder after the latter game. "Don, you sure as hell made a terrific adjustment this week, not having Fichtner to throw to. It really surprises the hell out of me how you get your timing down, working with different receivers every week."

Bob St. John of the *Dallas Morning News* remembered another incident in his biography of Tom Landry:

**Once [Bob] Hayes had been injured during a road game and on the return flight, Landry decided he'd move Gent from flanker to the other side, split end, where he'd**

**Washington Redskins great John Riggins finds a large hole in the Philadelphia defense in this 1979 game. When Riggins retired after the 1985 season he had virtually rewritten the rushing category of the Redskins record book, and he remains to this day their all-time rushing leader. He was elected to the Pro Football Hall of Fame in 1992.**

start against Philadelphia, instead of the injured Hayes. Landry walked to the back of the plane, the players' section, and found Gent.

"Pete," said Landry, "you'll be moving to the other side this week. So get ready."

"You mean, coach," said Pete, "that I'm going to play for Philadelphia?"

### VIOLATING THE SABBATH

This headline once appeared in New York City: "Sunday Football Goes to Court."

"I attend the games myself, and I fail to see any basis for such charges." With this statement Magistrate James Barrett in Washington Heights Court dismissed charges that players of the New York Giants and Cleveland Bulldogs professional football clubs violated Sabbath "blue laws" by playing on Sunday at the Polo Grounds. Summonses were handed to the captains and Dr. Harry March, sponsor of the local club, following a game at the Polo Grounds on November 1, 1925, but when the case came before him, Magistrate Barrett, on lack of evidence that the game disturbed the peace as was charged, dismissed the complaint.

## MISSPELLING

Halfback Don Kindt carried the ball for the Chicago Bears and played defensive back during the days of 60-minute men in the fifties. Like most Midway Monsters, he, at times, incurred the wrath of coach George Halas, who was never known to mince words. Kindt remembered this particular incident:

> We were playing at Wrigley Field. I was playing safety at the time . . . and Jug Girard, who had been my roommate at Wisconsin, was playing halfback for the Lions. Well, the Jugger ran a post-corner—that's where he runs toward the post and then cuts to the corner. Bobby Layne threw it to him, and we're just about at the goal line, and I dove and batted the ball into the air and knocked Jug on his butt at the same time. Well, the ball makes this little loop in the air and comes down right in Jug's gut.
>
> Halas was incensed, as he was known to get sometimes on the sideline. He ran all the way down to maybe the 10-yard line, where I was now standing right in front of the box where the mayor [Martin Kennelly] and his wife were sitting with some other local dignitaries. And he grabbed me and screamed at me, "You lousy cocksucker . . . you cunt!"
>
> And I said, "No, it's Kindt, coach. K-i-n-d-t. You pronounce it Kindt."

## SUBARASHI

Nippon Television Network (NTV) carried Super Bowl XXVI live to Japan. Because *amefuto*, or American football, remains in its infancy in the country, no famous football player was available for commentary.

So NTV hired one of its sports heroes, Tokyo Giants baseball player Shigeo Nagashima, who is Japan's equivalent of Willie Mays or Ted Williams.

Nagashima's favorite players seemed to be Redskins running back Earnest Byner and Redskins kicker Chip Lohmiller, both of whom he declared *subarashi*—marvelous.

## IT TAKES ALL KINDS

Takes all kinds . . . Consider this from an Associated Press wire story in 1941. Bert Bell was in his first year as a co-owner and head coach of the Steelers, after eight seasons as general manager and coach of the Eagles. Big Arthur Jarrett, by the way, did not make the team.

Bobby Beathard, one of professional football's most highly regarded administrators, served as general manager of the Washington Redskins from 1978 to 1988, during which time the Skins went to three Super Bowls, winning two of them, and to the playoffs five times. Beathard began his pro football career as a part-time scout for the Kansas City Chiefs in 1963; in 1972 he was named director of player personnel for the Miami Dolphins. After leaving the Redskins, Beathard served as general manager for the San Diego Chargers (1990–99). In 2002 he joined the Atlanta Falcons as senior adviser to the club's CEO.

**Washington Redskins owner George Preston Marshall, the "Big Chief," as he was sometimes called, liked to get into the spirit of things. Helping him don his headdress here is his wife, former motion picure star Corinne Griffith. Marshall launched the Redskins in Boston in 1932 and then took them to Washington; he ran the team until 1962 when ill health forced him to step down. Marshall is a charter member of the Pro Football Hall of Fame.**

HERSHEY, Pa. (AP), July 30—A 230-pound University of Hawaii graduate who gave up his job as assistant hangman of a penal colony to try out for the Pittsburgh Steelers' line this fall ought to make the grade if he gets used to wearing shoes on the gridiron.

Big Arthur Jarrett, who traveled 6,000 miles to this sports center to train with Bert Bell's new football squad, declared upon arrival it was just as easy to kick a ball with your bare feet. That's the way he did it with success in Hawaii.

Bell, however, ruled Arthur must wear regulation equipment and if necessary learn to kick with shoes on when the rest of the squad arrives Friday.

Bert is enthusiastic about this 23-year-old prospect and thinks he will land a guard or tackle assignment if he can conquer the shoe problem.

"He was recommended to us by a former Pitt player and if he is half as good as his record indicates, he will be one of the regulars when the National [Football] League season gets under way," says Bell, former owner of the Philadelphia Eagles.

**Where is the breakaway jersey when you need one? Washington backup quarterback Harry Theofiledes (No. 17) could surely use one in this game against the Dallas Cowboys. Trying to disrobe Theofiledes is Cowboys defensive end Jethro Pugh.**

**Jarrett's father was appointed warden of the penal colony on the island of Oahu, largest of the Hawaiian group, reports Bert. The boy went to live at the colony and when old enough was appointed a guard.**

**As a sort of promotion, Jarrett was made assistant hangman. The grinning athlete admits he never actually served in an execution, largely because the regular hangman always was on the job.**

## WELCOMINGS

After 10 straight losses in 1960, the Cowboys dueled the New York Giants to a 31–31 tie at Yankee Stadium in New York. The team flew back to Texas and was greeted at Dallas' Love Field by a party of two fans holding a sign that read: "Well Done, Cowboys."

As they walked into the airport, Tom Landry caught a glimpse of the two fans and turned to Tex Schramm, "Looks like we're making some progress," he said.

"Looks like we're making some progress."

—TOM LANDRY, AFTER A 31–31 TIE IN NEW YORK HALTED A 10-GAME LOSING STREAK IN 1960

Even a mountain of a man like Packer Ray Nitschke needs a little resuscitation from time to time. The heralded middle linebacker, who starred in college at Illinois, was the core around which Vince Lombardi fashioned his great defense in Green Bay in the sixties. An exceptional leader on the field and a ferocious competitor, Nitschke became a Pro Football Hall of Famer in 1978.

**A little sports mix-up in Washington. Redskins quarterback Harry Gilmer works out here with the Washington Senators circa 1950. The purpose of this exercise in sports blending has never been fully explained.**

In the *Dallas Morning News*, Sam Blair noted two years later:

> **When the team plane was forced to land at Memphis with mechanical trouble following a big victory in Washington, there was a memorable moment.**
>
> **It was a warm autumn evening in Dixie and once the pilot cut the engines at the far end of the ramp, there was only the sound of crickets when the door opened. Outside, sitting in a jeep, three maintenance men sat mutely.**
>
> **Before the first player could deplane, however, owner Clint Murchison Jr., rushed to the door.**
>
> **"Look sharp, men!" he yelled. "This may be our biggest welcome yet."**

## ADJUSTMENT

Darryl Carlton and Freddie Solomon, the Dolphins' first two draft choices in 1975, both from the University of Tampa, were being introduced to the South Florida media, and Dolphins' personnel chief Bobby Beathard couldn't contain his enthusiasm. "We had Carlton rated the number one offensive tackle in the country," Beathard was saying before he was interrupted.

"Let me warn you, Bobby, that's Bob Woolf standing over there," said head coach Don Shula. Woolf, the Boston attorney and most respected of NFL player agents, was handling Carlton's affairs.

Beathard cleared his throat. "This kid's green and has a long way to go," he said of Carlton. "It will be years and years before he's able to play."

### INTERLOPER

The Chicago Bears were moving toward a touchdown as time was running out in the first half during the NFL championship game of 1943 against the Washington Redskins. Ralph Brizzolara, acting president of the Bears while George Halas was in the navy, looked down the Bears bench and suddenly noticed that the person sitting at the end of it was not wearing a Bears uniform. He was, in fact, dressed in an elegant raccoon coat and homburg hat.

"My god, it's Marshall," Brizzolara shouted, as he stormed down to confront the owner of the Redskins. George Preston Marshall began to explain that he had merely been on his way down to the Redsksins' locker room and decided to pay a quick halftime visit to the Bears as well. Brizzolara, sure that Marshall was there for some nefarious purpose, like stealing signals or listening in on the Bears coaches' instructions, summoned Jack Goldie, the team's equipment manager. "Physically remove Marshall from this area," he told Jack.

Goldie clutched the fir-covered arm of the Redskins' owner and roughly escorted him back into the grandstand. There an usher demanded to see his ticket stub, which Marshall could not produce. The usher then called two policemen. Grasping Marshall by the arms, the lawmen were about to lead him from the ballpark when he finally managed to convince them that he actually was who he claimed he was.

After the game, Brizzolara said, "I didn't want Marshall eavesdropping. . . . A championship and a great honor were at stake. . . . That's the lowest way there can be of trying to win a game. . . . Yes, we threw him out—not invited him out."

Regarding the incident, Marshall said, "Fiddlesticks! It was a first-class, bush-league trick." And then he added, "You can say for me that Brizzolara is not a gentleman. And I'll never speak to him again."

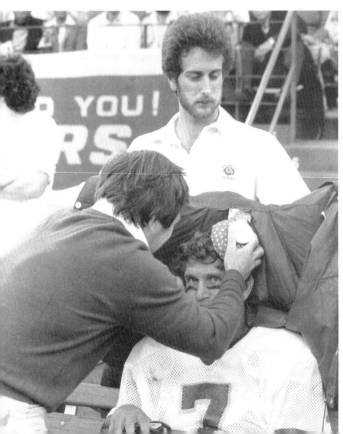

**No, it's not New Year's morning, and Joe Theismann is not suffering from a hangover. But the Redskins star does have a sore head in this 1984 photo. Theismann, from Notre Dame, was Washington's quarterback from 1974 through 1985.**

**George Preston Marshall's pride and joy, the Washington Redskins marching band. The band debuted in Washington in 1937 and over the years grew to a healthy 150-piece unit, much to the eternal happiness of the Redskins' owner.**

Later the following week, Elmer Layden, the NFL commissioner, also had something to say. He fined both Marshall and Brizzolara $500 each for "actions not reciprocal of the public confidence in the National Football League."

The Bears, incidentally, won the game, 41–21.

## THE PIGEON PROBLEM

Linebacker Ron McDole told this story of when he was playing for Buffalo:

We had a tough game that week and [Bills' head coach Lou] Saban wanted to put in some new stuff. But when we hit the practice field at War Memorial Stadium we found maybe a thousand pigeons grazing. We shouted and made noise, and the pigeons gave up one-half of the practice field, but we never did scare enough of them away. So after about 30 minutes Saban had to call it quits. But the coach vowed he'd get his friends in the police department to take care of the situation the next day.

The next afternoon as we hit the practice field there were four police sharpshooters picking off the pigeons one by one. Well, you can imagine that was crazy. Every time a shot went off, a lineman would jump offside. Saban was beside himself and finally had to call practice off after about 20 minutes of shooting.

Pittsburgh Steelers quarterback Bobby Layne (No. 32) is almost obscured by leaping Dallas Cowboys defensive end George Andrie (No. 66) here. No one played harder on and off the field than Texas All-American Layne, who left his mark on the NFL by his great quarterbacking for the Detroit Lions, whom he joined after a year with the Bears and another with the New York Bulldogs. He led the Lions to four divisional titles and three NFL championships in his nine years there. His last tour of NFL duty was with the Steelers (1958–62). As much as he loved to party, he always came through on game day. Layne was inducted into the Pro Football Hall of Fame in 1967.

The police suggested he call in the health department. They did, and poison seed was laid down on the field late that afternoon. Saban figured he had the problem licked.

But guess what? The next afternoon when we hit the practice field it was covered with a thousand dead pigeons, and we spent the entire workout picking up the pigeons one by one and disposing of them. Saban went ape.

"The next afternoon when we hit the practice field it was covered with a thousand dead pigeons. . . ."

—BUFFALO LINEBACKER RON MCDOLE

## THE "PERFECT" PLAY

Jack Ferrante was a pass-catching end on a Philadelphia Eagles team that filed into old Shibe Park on December 19, 1948, in the middle of a snowstorm to meet the then Chicago Cardinals for the NFL title. He had played with distinction. He was a pro. At the end of the day, in point of fact, he would be a member of a world championship team because the Eagles would win 7–0.

But that would hardly be the full reason Jack Ferrante would remember that day.

All week long, the Eagles had been driven by the thought that if they could stun the Cardinals at the outset, they could win. The plan was to hit with an enormous surprise bomb at the start, then use the steady, time-consuming running of Steve Van Buren to control the game. The play they chose to trigger this strategy was called "81 special," and it was designed to combine the talents of Ferrante and quarterback Tommy Thompson.

And so it went. Thompson dropped back to pass through the swirling snow. Savage blocking held the Cardinals' defenders in check. Ferrante whizzed by the secondary, a kind of Hermes in shoulder pads. Thompson threw a strike. Ferrante made a picture-perfect catch . . . 65 yards . . . touchdown . . . drums were beaten . . . frost-bitten bugles belched . . . players hugged each other . . . and back at the line of scrimmage a guy in a striped shirt was standing with his hands on his hips calling for the ball.

"Eagles offside."

Ferrante leaped high in the air, slipped on the snowy turf, regained his balance, and raced toward the official. He had been part of perfection. Men rarely get that chance. And now stupidity had thrown

John "Bull" Doehring was unique in that he, on occasion, would throw behind-the-back passes. Playing for the Bears in the thirties, he was never the starting quarterback, but when he got into the game, well, surprises happened. In one game he flipped a behind-the-back pass 30 yards to end Luke Johnsos standing alone in the end zone who was "so astonished that I dropped the ball, even though it landed right in my hands." It was also said that Doehring's arm was so strong that he never threw a pass as far as he could because no receiver was fast enough to get far enough downfield to catch it.

perfection for a five-yard loss. Some bit player had slipped between Thompson and Ferrante on the one hand and destiny on the other.

"Who . . . who . . . who the hell was it?" Ferrante demanded, sputtering in the official's frosty face.

"You," the man with the whistle said.

### SUPERSTITIONS, MIAMI STYLE

A reporter in the seventies asked—timidly—of the Miami Dolphins if it was true that one of the players wore red bikinis underneath his uniform.

And he learned that one indeed did—linebacker Bob Matheson, who considered it good luck.

He then learned further that there was no shortage of other superstitions among the supermen who had won Super Bowls VII and VIII.

If his kicking clicked, Garo Yepremian wouldn't change his shoes. But if he missed one, he gave away the "unlucky shoes."

Linebackers Tim Foley (because he was Irish) and Nick Buoniconti (because he went to Notre Dame) both wore shamrocks on the outside of their helmets. And the don of the Dolphins, Coach Shula, insisted on occupying the same seat every time he stepped into a plane, registered at the same hotel, and said "Good luck tomorrow" to his men at the same time before every game. And when the going was good, he wouldn't permit players to change roommates.

### THE BAND SILENCED

The Washington Redskins band, at least according to recorded history, was silenced only once. And it was the night of one of the team's most glorious victories.

For the last game of the 1937 regular season at the Polo Grounds, one

**Elroy "Crazy Legs" Hirsch got his nickname because of his unorthodox style of running, but it didn't hinder him on the football field. To the contrary, he was one of the game's greatest receivers: fast, surehanded, and a dazzling runner once he gathered in a pass. Out of Wisconsin (where he would return later as athletic director), Hirsch first joined the Chicago Rockets of the AAFC, but he moved to the Los Angeles Rams in 1949 for an illustrious nine-year career hauling in passes from Hall of Famers Bob Waterfield and Norm Van Brocklin. Hirsch himself entered the Pro Football Hall of Fame in 1968.**

Fumbles, fumbles, everywhere. The elusive football squirts out of the hands of Chicago Bears quarterback Johnny Lujack (top photo) in a 1948 game at Wrigley Field. Same franchise, 19 years later (bottom photo): Bears quarterback Jack Concannon watches the ball squirt out toward a Redskins defender; the Bears lost the football while the unidentified Redskins tackler lost his helmet.

that would decide the NFL East title that year, Marshall brought his marching band along with the team to New York. The band, all wearing white headdresses and appropriate Indian costumes, marched down Seventh Avenue in Manhattan with the Big Chief at the head of it. Inside the Polo Grounds, its rendition of "Hail to the Redskins" so inspired the team that it decimated the Giants 49–14, thus earning the right to play in the NFL title game against the Bears.

After the game, the band, the team, Marshall, and his entourage boarded the last train back to Washington. At Union Station in Washington at about 11:00 that

**Jimmy Conzelman: quarterback, coach, team owner, raconteur, actor, songwriter, and piano player. He was all of those and more. Conzelman played for five different teams in the twenties: the Decatur Staleys, Rock Island Independents, Milwaukee Badgers, Detroit Panthers, and Providence Steam Roller. He coached several of the teams he played on but is best remembered for the years he guided the Chicago Cardinals (1940–42, 1946–48) and the NFL championship he led them to in 1947. His overall coaching stats are 87–63–17. Dapper Jimmy joined the Pro Football Hall of Fame in 1964.**

This hardly looks like the style of the game's first great pass receiver. But it is Green Bay Packer Don Hutson in a 1940 game against the Pittsburgh Pirates. Hutson, whose style was ordinarily sublime, commandeered every pass-receiving record in the game during his 11 years with Green Bay (1935–45) and was a deadly accurate place-kicker. He is a charter member of the Pro Football Hall of Fame. Chasing Hutson here is Pirates defensive back Merl Condit.

night, some ten thousand fans were waiting to welcome home the victors. Marshall thought it only proper for his beloved band to lead a little march up Pennsylvania Avenue.

The Washington police, less musically inclined than Marshall was, especially just before midnight, told him that he could not stage his victory march without an official city license. Marshall argued vehemently with them. The police stood firm: "No license, no parade."

Marshall left angrily, but not in defeat. He marshaled as many members of the band as he could find and guided them up the avenue, out of sight of the police—at least so he thought. There they would march a single block to the tune of "Hail to the Redskins."

As the first few bars of that famous fight song lilted into the balmy Washington night air, the police reappeared. The music stopped, and the police threatened to arrest the entire band. But, having only one patrol wagon with them, they settled for merely collaring the drum major.

A deprived, frustrated Marshall grumped that hostile New York had allowed his band to march on *its* streets while his own hometown was denying him and his triumphal team that very same, simple honor. But to no avail. He followed the paddy wagon down to First Precinct headquarters and came up with the $25 to bail his drum major out of jail.

"The way this game's going, I had to down a few at halftime."

—LIONS QUARTERBACK BOBBY LAYNE

### HALFTIME REFRESHMENT

Baltimore Colts Hall of Fame tackle Art Donovan told this one:

**We were going against [Bobby] Layne again, only this time he was with the Lions. It was late in the third quarter, and we were putting a helluva lot of pressure on him. He**

**was screaming at his offensive lineman, kicking their shins in the huddle, that kind of thing. And we were all watching him do this from our defensive huddle and busting a gut laughing. He was a wild man over there. Finally Detroit broke their huddle, snapped the ball, and as Bobby dropped back to pass, I hit him a shot, and he went down. I was lying over him and he smelled like an empty wine bottle. I said to him, "Jesus, Bobby, you goddamn reek. You must have downed quite a few last night."**

**He just looked up at me with this silly grin and said, "Fatso, let me let you in on a secret. The way this game's going, I had to down a few at halftime."**

### CRAZY LEGS

It was the final game of the 1954 season. The Rams were playing Green Bay at home. Elroy "Crazy Legs" Hirsch previously had announced it would be his final appearance in a Rams uniform. When the gun went off at the end of the game, thousands of youngsters raced out onto the field and surrounded him. They began tugging at his uniform. His jersey, bearing the familiar No. 40, was quickly torn to shreds. His pants were next to go, followed by his shoulder and hip pads. If the postgame show had been on television, it would have been rated X. Finally, reduced to only a skimpy athletic supporter, Elroy Hirsch trotted off the Coliseum field, tears streaming down his face.

### BUBBLES CASH HAD AN OBSESSION

Occasionally, ladies get into the act at pro football games. There is the case of Bubbles Cash, who will go into the National Football League record book with the following statistics: 46–23–40. Professionally she was what you might call a dancer. That is to say, she marched back and forth to music while her costume magically fell away. Her football career was about as brief as her work clothes.

Absolutely denying any intent to disrupt games or draw attention to herself, she broke up the action at a Cowboys game in the Cotton Bowl, a Chiefs game at Kansas City's Municipal Stadium, and an Oilers game at Rice Stadium. It was an uncontrollable impulse, she explained.

She claimed that she would be sitting there quietly in her $10 box seat when suddenly she would be seized with the urge to kiss one of the players. In each instance, her press agent would come galloping up behind her, ready to give her name to any eager newspaper reporter. Bubbles met defeat in New Orleans, where strippers are probably better understood. Someone discovered the name of the lady who was undressing at the joint *across* the street from the establishment where

"Joe Carr, the head of the NFL . . . said the franchise fee was a thousand dollars, but he'd let me have Detroit for 50 dollars."

—JIMMY CONZELMAN ON HOW HE OBTAINED THE OLD DETROIT PANTHERS

NFL heroes as movie stars. Film critics suggested they'd be wise to stick to football.

Bubbles did her nightly routine. Bubbles was warned in advance that if she placed one pretty pedicured toe on the turf at a Saints home game, it would be announced to the press that the pretty trespasser was really Miss Violet Dare. Rather than give aid, comfort, and publicity to the competition, Bubbles retired from pro football.

## SHOW BIZ

Jimmy Conzelman, Hall of Fame halfback and heralded raconteur, often liked to recount how he had obtained the franchise of the old Detroit Panthers and tell of his somewhat unorthodox plan to promote the ballclub:

In 1925, Joe Carr, the head of the NFL, asked me to bring pro football to Detroit. He said the franchise fee was a thousand dollars, but he'd let me have Detroit for 50 dollars. I said fine, and suddenly I was the owner, coach, and only player for the Panthers. But I got together a team and uncorked a plan to make them well known.

My plan was to get Notre Dame's fabled Four Horsemen for the team. Not only would they play football for us, but I would work out a vaudeville act and the four of them and myself would take it on the road before and after the season. I talked to them and they were for it, so I lined up some theatrical agents to work out the details.

I was to be the piano player. Harry Stuhldreher was a pretty good singer, and he was going to sing a song called "She's a Mean Job." Jim Crowley planned to do a clog dance and had a routine for a comic monologue. The problem was that Elmer Layden and Don Miller didn't have an act, so we took some time to see if we could get them to do a song or some kind of routine. Time went by and finally Layden called me up and told me he had agreed to take a job with some recreation department and to count him out. I didn't think we could make it as "The Three Horsemen and Conzelman"; neither did the theatrical agents, and so the whole idea fell apart.

## PLAYING THE GOAL POST

In 1942, Green Bay's Don Hutson set an NFL record by catching 17 touchdown passes. He was also in the midst of setting a record for touchdown passes in consecutive games when he ran up against the Chicago Bears at Wrigley Field.

The Bears, a powerhouse that would not lose any of their 11 games that year, were winning 38–0 in the fourth quarter. Bears coach George Halas, secure in his impending victory, was also

**Dutch Clark, better known for his talents as a player, coached the Detroit Lions in 1937 and 1938, then piloted the Philadelphia Eagles from 1939 to 1942. His record of 30–34–2 pales in comparison to that of his namesake (but not relation) Potsy Clark, who coached the Portsmouth Spartans, Detroit Lions, and Brooklyn Dodgers during the thirties and compiled a record of 64–42–12.**

determined to snap Hutson's touchdown-reception streak, remembering no doubt how Hutson had burned the Bears so often in the past.

With two minutes left in the game, Green Bay had no chance to win. But they were on the Bears, 20-yard line and trying to keep Hutson's record alive. Cecil Isbell threw three straight incompletions, principally because Hutson was covered by three Bears defenders: George McAfee, Harry Clark, and Dante Magnani. But on fourth down! Pat Livingston, sports editor of the *Pittsburgh Press,* described it aptly:

> **Then came the most incredible premeditated play I ever saw on a football field. . . . Lining up as a flanker, harassed by three Bears, the cagey old Alabaman ran a simple post pattern, diagonally in on the twin-poled uprights, Bears convoying him, stride by stride.**
>
> **As the four men raced under the bar, Hutson hooked his elbow around the upright, stopped abruptly, flung his body sharply left, and left the red-faced Bears scrambling around their cleats. He stood alone in the end zone as he casually gathered Isbell's throw to his chest.**

## GIFFORD'S VISITOR

While Frank Gifford was having his injured knee attended to in a New York hospital in 1958, he awoke at about 5:30 one morning to find a large, trembling young man at the foot of his bed. The immobilized Gifford watched as the man shook the bed and ranted, "What's the matter with your Giants? What's the matter with you, Gifford?"

The man walked over to the venetian blinds and ran his hand up and down them to make noise. "What you need is someone like me, a killer. I was in Korea."

Gifford grabbed the water pitcher beside his bed. "If he was going to come at me I was going to gong him," Gifford said later. The man didn't, but he also did not leave. He just stood there, running his hand along the blinds.

Gifford finally said to him, "If you really think you can help the team, get your ass down to Yankee Stadium. Tell them what you can do." The man sort of nodded and left, much to Gifford's relief.

However, the man did take the Giff's advice and went to Yankee Stadium. He managed to get into the locker room, where most of the players by that time were suiting up for practice, and began screaming, first at 260-pound Dick Modzelewski and then at some others. According to sportswriter Barry Gottherer, the man then began drop-kicking footballs around the room, castigating the team before several policemen arrived to take him away.

As he was leaving, Gottherer quoted him as shouting back, "All right, so you don't appreciate me. I'll go down to Baltimore and help Johnny Unitas out."

## JUNGLE JAMEY

In 1960, as the Cowboys convened that first summer out at Forest Grove, Oregon, one of the people to arrive was a barefoot place-kicker, who, as it turned out, had a variety of other eccentricities as well. Sam Blair, in his book *Dallas Cowboys, Pro or Con?,* tells the story best of the amusing anomaly who had nick-named himself Jungle Jamey:

Portland was the home of James Bacilerri, which meant it was only a short drive out to the Dallas camp in his battered 1949 Ford, which was covered with autographs and had a hunk of bear meat swinging from the radio aerial. Proximity meant nothing to Jungle Jamey, however. He had traveled the entire country in pursuit of his two greatest pleasures: visiting his favorite teams and gate-crashing. He was capable of turning up anywhere. . . .

You knew right away that Jamey wasn't just another guy who dropped by to watch practice. A stocky man in his middle thirties, he wore a white hunter's hat with a snakeskin band, ragged short pants, a football jersey bearing number 22, and he was barefoot. Oh, yes, he had a large white rabbit on a leash. He called the rabbit "Texas Freeloader." Jungle Jamey and his rabbit soon were leading the players out of the locker room to the practice field, where he would try a few barefoot field goals and dispense a lot of advice. . . . But it was inevitable that Jamey soon would be at odds with Tex Schramm. Jamey claimed that Schramm shouldn't be there and was disturbed that Tex had so much authority and yet was neither coaching nor playing. Schramm had different ideas about who was out of place. . . .

Intriguing character though he was, Jamey added nothing to the camp in Schramm's opinion. Several nights, Tex was ready to evict him but couldn't find him. One night, Schramm got down on his hands and knees in the recreation room and looked under a grand piano, where Jamey sometimes slept. But that was one of the nights that Jamey went to the stadium and slept on the 50-yard line. . . .

Landry had no objection to Jamey, and he talked Schramm into letting him stay. He was still there the first weekend in August, when the Cowboys flew to Seattle for their first exhibition game. Jamey was on the plane.

Fritz Hawn had arrived earlier and decided there should be a band to meet the team at the airport. He hired some musicians and gave them a large sign, "Jungle Jamey's Jazz Band." As the Cowboys left the plane, they played happily and nodded to Jamey.

"They ought to tighten the immigration laws."

—VIKING COACH NORM VAN BROCKLIN, FOLLOWING A 32–31 LOSS TO DETROIT AND SIX FIELD GOALS BY KICKER GARO YEPREMIAN

### SORE LOSER

In 1966, Detroit kicker Garo Yepremian booted six field goals in one game, tying the then NFL record, to lead the Lions to a 32–31 victory over Minnesota. Asked after the game his feelings about the performance, Vikings coach Norm Van Brocklin responded, "They ought to tighten the immigration laws."

### THE WORD FROM THE CLARKS

The Detroit Lions had two different Clarks coaching them in the earlier days: Potsy, from 1931 to 1936 and in 1940; and Dutch, 1937 and 1938. According to *Lions Pride: 60 Years of Detroit Lions Football,* each had his own theory on training.

Head coach George "Potsy" Clark urged his players to run barefoot prior to training camp, hoping the players' feet would become tough enough to absorb the pain caused by new shoes.

In a letter sent to his players before the start of the 1937 training camp, head coach Earl "Dutch" Clark urged his players to get as much sun as possible but to stay out of the water. "Every player will be expected to report with a good coat of tan over his whole body," wrote Clark. But "Swimming is not a good conditioning exercise."

**Baltimore Colts great Johnny Unitas is caught in a pensive moment on the sideline in this photograph. Unquestionably one of the greatest quarterbacks ever to play the pro game, Unitas, out of Louisville, was drafted and waived by the Pittsburgh Steelers in 1955 but was finally picked up as an afterthought by the Colts. He went on to rewrite the NFL passing record book during his 17 years with Baltimore (1956–72), played a final year with the San Diego Chargers, and was ushered into the Pro Football Hall of Fame in 1979.**

### INACCURATE PASSING, PERHAPS

In a little pregame hype before an Oakland-Baltimore game in 1980, Raiders quarterback Dan Pastorini put on a passing exhibition before the assembled press and media outside the hotel where the Oakland players were staying. He stood in the parking lot and hurled the ball up to a sixth-floor balcony.

When told of this feat, former Colts great Johnny Unitas put it in perspective: "Yeah, but his receivers were on the second floor."

Packers greats at work in the sixties: Jim Taylor (No. 31), after a handoff from Bart Starr (No. 15), follows guard Jerry Kramer into enemy territory.

# 6

## Personalities

Q: Have you ever bet on football games?

A: Yes, I have bet on ballgames.

Q: On games in which you were playing?

A: Yes, I have.

**I**f football is drama—and there is no question it is dramatic—it can be said the players are the actors and the coaches the directors. And to continue the metaphor, the ensemble cast is enormous, with an almost endless array of characters, from leading men to varying character roles and often just cameo appearances. The show goes on at Sunday matinees, Monday nights, and later in each season on Saturdays and Thursdays. The script is set at each performance, and each is different from the one before and the one that will follow. Maybe it's not Shakespeare or Chekhov, nor Tennessee Williams or David Mamet, but still it stands as first-rate drama with memorable performers.

Over the decades since the start of the Roaring Twenties, the game of professional football has produced an abundance of legends: names like Thorpe, Grange, Nagurski, and Hutson; Baugh, Luckman, and Graham; Layne, Hornung, and Brown; Butkus, Nitschke, and Marchetti; Unitas, Staubach, and Bradshaw—the list goes on and on.

Each team has its unforgettable litany of stars of the past. Who could think of the Giants and not remember Frank Gifford, Sam Huff, Lawrence Taylor, or Phil Simms; or the Packers and Bart Starr, Willie Davis, or Jim Taylor; the Cowboys and Don Meredith, Tony Dorsett, and Randy White; the Browns and Marion Motley, Lou Groza, and Dante Lavelli; the Rams and Bob Waterfield, Norm Van Brocklin, Elroy Hirsch, and Merlin Olsen; the Redskins and Sonny Jurgensen, Charley Taylor, John Riggins, and Art Monk; the Bears and Bulldog Turner, Gale Sayers, Walter Payton, and Mike Singletary; the Steelers and Mean Joe Greene, Jack Lambert, and Franco Harris; the Lions and Doak Walker, Joe Schmidt, and Barry Sanders; the 49ers and Hugh McElhenny, John Brodie, Joe Montana, and Jerry Rice; the Dolphins and Larry Csonka, Bob Griese, and Dan Marino; the Raiders and George Blanda, Gene Upshaw, Ken Stabler, and Fred Biletnikoff; and many, many more?

They have left their marks on the game and in the memories of the legions of fans who cheered them on over the years. Their personalities are as diverse as their individual talents. From party animal to straight arrow, their spirit and their exploits on and off the field have become the lore of the National Football League.

The directors in the drama are equally as diverse: "Papa Bear" George Halas and his patented rages on the sideline; Vince Lombardi and the fear and awe he struck in the hearts of his players; Paul Brown guiding the reintegration of blacks into the NFL; the subdued faces of Bud Grant and Tom Landry on the sideline; the quiet intensity of Don Shula and Joe Gibbs; and the not-so-quiet intensity of Bill Parcells and Mike Ditka.

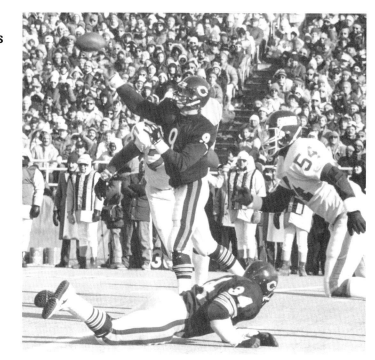

**Bears quarterback Jim McMahon gets off a pass in the 1985 playoff game against the Giants. The brash, outspoken McMahon was also an effective team leader and instrumental in the Bears' sweep to that year's NFL title. On the ground is Hall of Fame halfback Walter Payton (No. 34), and pursuing McMahon is Hall of Fame linebacker Lawrence Taylor. The Bears destroyed the Giants that day, 21–0.**

Together, performers and coaches, they fill the drama with color, excitement, laughter, and sometimes a tear or two. And we, the audience, are entertained royally.

WOWING LONDON

Jimmy Conzelman, one of the great early halfbacks, played for four different teams during the twenties and later coached the Chicago Cardinals to the NFL championship in 1947. He loved to tell this story:

After the 1922 season the Milwaukee Badgers offered me $200 if I could come up there and coach and play for their club. . . .

My first job . . . was to look over the material we had and let some of the players go. One of the players I let go after several weeks was Paul Robeson.

I had played against Robeson when he was at Rutgers and I was at Great Lakes. He had been a one-man team, throwing and catching passes, punting, and even playing tackle on offense at times. But he was sick of football by the time we met in Milwaukee and wasn't going to be much use to us as a player. He was valuable as a member of the singing quartet we had, although the other members didn't think much of his voice.

On the day he left I asked him what he was going to do and he said, "I don't know, but I might go to New York and try show business." A few years later I read in an eastern newspaper he was wowing London as the male lead in *Show Boat.*

### SIGNING IS SUCH SWEET SORROW

*Brash* became a synonym for Jim McMahon, who joined the Chicago Bears in 1982 and quarterbacked them to a Super Bowl championship three years later (Super Bowl XX). Outrageous, some said, but petulant or annoying or simply telling it like it is, he was always entertaining. He talked of signing with the Bears his rookie year:

> After I was drafted by the Bears, they brought me to Chicago with all the hoopla to meet everybody—the organization people, the press, and the other media. I don't remember exactly when it was that I first met George Halas—sometime later during contract negotiations. I think he probably wasn't too happy with me or my agent around that time. But when I did meet him, he basically told me that I was too small, I had a bad arm, a bad knee, that I couldn't see very well, and I ought to just go to Canada, because I wouldn't make it in the NFL. If I got $200 a game, I'd be overpaid.

**Chicago Cardinals Hall of Fame halfback Charlie Trippi breaks one here in a game at the since-demolished Comiskey Park in the late forties. An All-American at Georgia, Trippi was drafted by the Cardinals in 1947 and joined what was dubbed the "Dream Backfield," consisting of quarterback Paul Christman, halfback Marshall Goldberg (subsequently replaced by Elmer Angsman), and fullback Pat Harder. Trippi was the star of the '47 NFL title game in which the Cards defeated the Philadelphia Eagles, 28–21, scoring touchdowns on a 44-yard run from scrimmage and a 75-yard punt return. Trippi played nine seasons for Chicago and was enshrined in the Pro Football Hall of Fame in 1968.**

**At any rate, he offered me a contract, which was horse shit. . . . I remember too, when I did sign the contract, [McMahon's agent Jerry] Argovitz and I gave them a piece of paper that said we reserved the right to sue the Bears because I was signing under duress. And that, I think, got both Halas and Jim Finks pretty pissed off.**

### WIN SOME, LOSE SOME

George Preston Marshall, the super showman and owner of the Washington Redskins, had fought all of the league in an effort to get the goal posts moved from 10 yards back to the goal line in an effort to put more scoring and, thus, more entertainment value into the game.

Marshall won.

Marshall lost.

If that sounds confusing, then consider: December 16, 1945. The Rams were still playing out of Cleveland. Marshall's Redskins met them for the title. Cleveland won 15–14. And why did Cleveland win?

Well, in the very first period, the Redskins held the Rams on the Washington 5 to shut down a Cleveland scoring threat. Two plays later, Sammy Baugh dropped

**William "Refrigerator" Perry, the Chicago Bears' 325-pound (plus, many added) defensive tackle, turned fullback here, scored a touchdown in this 1985 game against the Packers to break a 7–7 tie at Soldier Field, leading to a 23–7 victory. Behind Perry is quarterback Jim McMahon who handed off to him.**

back in his own end zone to pass. Downfield, end Wayne Millner had broken into the clear. Baugh released the ball. The ball went forward. The ball came backward. Incredibly, it had struck the goal post.

What followed was total confusion. They sent for a rule book, which clearly stated at that time that because the ball had not left the end zone, the play was ruled a safety. Two points for Cleveland. Enough to make the difference. Marshall's legislative hand had put the posts between Baugh and Millner and backfired on him.

### GOOD-BYE JOHNNY BLOOD

In 1934, Johnny Blood McNally, the "Vagabond Halfback," as he enjoyed being called, was abruptly traded by Green Bay to the Pittsburgh Pirates. Here's how it came about, as the charter Hall of Famer recalled:

> Actually, in the long run, I guess I didn't get along so well [with Packers coach Curly Lambeau] because he finally fired me. On paper I was sold to the Pittsburgh team, but he really fired me. It came after several of us had been out one night. . . . We were out *all* night as a matter of fact. Well, I went directly to practice in the morning, got all suited up. Lambeau was looking at me kind of funny as I remember. Anyway, I tried to punt the ball, missed it, and fell flat on my ass. Lambeau told me to get the hell off the field, and after practice was over he told me he was getting rid of me.
>
> I came back to Green Bay a year later and Lambeau took me back, but we never got along very well after that.

### THE BEST PUNT RETURNER YOU NEVER HEARD OF

According to *The Pro Football Chronicle*, by Dan Daly and Bob O'Donnell, the greatest punt returner in NFL history was a 5'5", 145-pound dynamo named Two Bits Homan, also known as Babe Homan. "A manikin in moleskins," the newspapers called him. "A shrimp in armor." "Midget." "Dwarf."

Henry Homan played quarterback (blocking back) and safety for the Frankford Yellow Jackets from 1925 to 1930, years when no official records were kept. But the most reliable source on the subject, *The Sports Encyclopedia: Pro Football,* puts him at the top of the punt-return heap with a 13.59-yard average on 82 runbacks. That's almost a yard better than George McAfee (12.78) and Jack Christiansen (12.75), currently ranked one and two on the league's "all-time" list.

One of the NFL's all-time great running backs, Dallas Cowboy Tony Dorsett steps out in Super Bowl XII here; Dorsett scored the Cowboys' first touchdown that day in the 27–10 Dallas rout of the Denver Broncos. An All-American at Pittsburgh, Dorsett joined the Cowboys in 1977 and starred in the backfield through the 1987 season, capturing virtually every team rushing record (most were later displaced by Emmitt Smith). He was elected to the Pro Football Hall of Fame in 1994.

Two longtime Texas friends, who played against each other in college—Doak Walker at Southern Methodist University and Bobby Layne with Texas, both All-Americans—were also on the same team in the NFL. Both came to the Detroit Lions in 1950; Walker, shown carrying the ball above in a 1955 game against the Chicago Bears, retired after the 1955 season; Layne was traded in 1958. Both are in the Pro Football Hall of Fame, Layne entering in 1967 and Walker in 1986.

Homan's style was unique for its time. He used to catch punts going full speed—no easy trick given the size of the ball (not to mention the size of his hands) and the windy conditions common in the days before large stadiums.

"Every move Homan makes is colorful," a Philadelphia sportswriter said. "The spectators look for this midget to perform some spectacular feat every time he takes a step whether or not he has the ball."

Two Bits somehow survived six seasons in the rough-and-tumble NFL. He later coached high school football in Glens Falls, New York, and was inducted posthumously into the Pennsylvania Sports Hall of Fame in 1969.

### A HALL OF FAMER, NONETHELESS

Dallas linebacker Thomas "Hollywood" Henderson liked to make it clear that he was not especially fond of the Pittsburgh Steelers, a team the Cowboys were in constant contention with for NFL titles in the seventies, most especially Pittsburgh

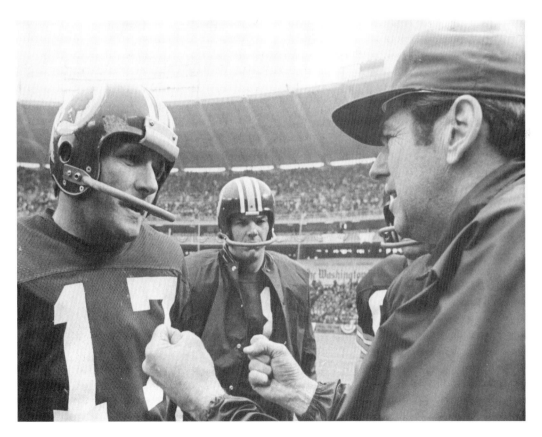

**Quarterback Billy Kilmer (No. 17) confers with coach George Allen on the Washington Redskins sideline at RFK Stadium in 1972. Looking on is backup quarterback Sam Wyche.**

middle linebacker Jack Lambert, about whom he had this to say: "I don't care for the man. He makes more money than I do, and he don't have no teeth."

### SCREWED

Before Super Bowl IX, Vikings tackle Ron Yary and Steelers defensive end L. C. Greenwood were engaged in a fiery intercamp exchange. As Greenwood was demonstrating some of his moves to a group of sportswriters, he slammed into an easy chair that wouldn't budge. "It's screwed into the floor," Greenwood said. "That's more like it. I'm so fast Yary's gonna think *he* was screwed into the ground."

"The only similarity between me and that chair," Yary replied, "is that Greenwood will be spending a lot of time on his seat."

### KILMER ON MCDOLE

"[Redskins linebacker Ron] McDole's storytelling is so amusing that if I were president of U.S. Steel I'd give the guy $200,000 a year just to hang around me and entertain everyone," recalled Redskins' quarterback Billy Kilmer.

As an example, McDole recalled the week he tore up his knee for the Redskins:

**Ollie Matson starred for the Chicago Cardinals (1952, 1954–58), the Los Angeles Rams (1959–62), the Detroit Lions (1963), and the Philadelphia Eagles (1964–66). He made it to the Pro Football Hall of Fame in 1972.**

OLLIE MATSON
CONSIDERED TOP
RUNNING BACK
IN PRO GAME

*Fred Reinert*
PLAIN DEALER

I made the mistake of hurting my knee the same week Larry Brown hurt his. We had an important game the next week, and I wanted to play although my kneecap rolled like jelly. The Redskins had seven doctors, and all of them were working on Larry Brown. I didn't mind that. It figured. After all, Larry was the stud running back, and we needed him in the game.

But I got worried when it was 10 minutes before we took the field for pregame warm-ups and nobody had taped my knee. I raised my hand like you do in school and tried to get somebody's attention. Nobody bothered.

So I took my stool and inched it over to where they were working on

Larry. Finally I just put my leg in between Larry's hoping some tape might accidentally get wrapped on my knee.

But one of the doctors yelled, "What's that white leg doing in here?" and I pulled back.

Finally as they were herding us out onto the field, one of the trainers spied me and started wrapping my knee as we ran through the tunnel. The moral is never get hurt the same week as a star running back.

A great catch by one of the game's most underrated pass receivers, Jim Benton of the Los Angeles Rams, in a 1946 game against the Chicago Bears at the L.A. Coliseum. Always in the shadow of the great end Don Hutson, Benton, whose college was Arkansas, played all but one year with the Rams (six while they were still in Cleveland) and never got the recognition he deserved. When he retired after the 1947 season, Benton was second only to Hutson in the major pass-reception categories of the NFL record book. In the background is Chicago Bears great Bulldog Turner (No. 66).

## TERRY BRADSHAW

Money was tighter in football in the seventies, as illustrated by this story from Pittsburgh Steelers great Terry Bradshaw in his autobiography *It's Only a Game*.

> I didn't even have an agent [in 1970, the year Bradshaw joined the Steelers]. A lot of players didn't have agents then; we couldn't understand why we should pay an agent a commission for not getting us the same salary we couldn't get on our own. Owners were tougher then, and players had much less negotiating power. The agents today earn more money for negotiating rookie contracts than I made for playing. When I got drafted, my father and his lawyer sat down at a table and met with every agent who wanted to represent me. Eventually they eliminated each of them, and my father represented me. I was real proud of him for doing it for me. Poor, but

Cleveland Browns guard Bill Willis (No. 74) charges into a pileup here, a place in which he was most commonly in the middle. An Ohio State star, Willis joined Marion Motley on the Browns in 1946 in the AAFC and helped pave the way for blacks in the NFL. With four years in the AAFC and four more in the NFL, Willis, a great blocker and a formidable middle guard on defense, was a perennial All-Pro. He was inducted into the Pro Football Hall of Fame in 1977.

proud. My dad didn't know what he was doing, and the Steelers helped him do it. The only things that interfered with my father's ability to be an effective agent were his honesty and his ethics. He wouldn't even consider holding me out for several months for a better contract, which definitely cut down on our negotiating position.

Looking back, I really was the perfect draft choice; I wanted to play pro football so desperately I probably would have played for nothing—although if I had made that offer, the Steelers probably would have offered me 20 percent less.

Bradshaw finally signed a five-year deal: a $110,000 bonus spread over ten years and a $25,000 salary that escalated $5,000 a year.

### A THOUGHT TO REMEMBER

John Wilbur, an offensive lineman for the Cowboys (1966–69), Rams (1970), and Redskins (1971–74), was quoted in *Sports Illustrated* regarding the Washington-Dallas rivalry:

It got to you. I mean, he [George Allen] never referred to the Dallas Cowboys without calling them the goddamn Dallas Cowboys. I can't think of them as anything else now. My nine-year-old son, Nathan, even calls them that.

**The Chicago Bears' Doug Atkins (No. 81), on his knees in this game at Wrigley Field in the sixties, proved to be one of the most feared defensive linemen of the era. He was forever in confrontation with owner/coach George Halas, but the two shared a mutual respect for each other, in football terms anyway.**

**Sonny Jurgensen (No. 9) leads the Washington Redskins onto the field in 1972. To his right is coach George Allen. This team, about to take on the Giants in New York (the Skins would win, 23–16), would make it to the Super Bowl, but there they would fall to the undefeated Miami Dolphins, 14–7.**

### FUNNY YOU SHOULD SAY THAT

New Orleans quarterback Archie Manning spent a particularly harrowing afternoon escaping the charges of Los Angeles defensive tackle Merlin Olsen. Afterward, Manning said, "Damn! He's like a state fair. He gets bigger and better every year."

After St. Louis had upended Washington in a tense struggle, Cardinals running back Jim Otis said, "That was a Dial soap game. It took the worry out of being close."

Broadcaster Howard Cosell asked New York Jets quarterback Joe Namath how many great broadcasters there were, and Namath said, "One less than you think, Howard."

### ART ROONEY

Pittsburgh Steelers owner and Pro Football Hall of Famer Art Rooney, as quoted in Myron Cope's classice *The Game That Was*, remembered an incident involing "blue laws."

In 1933 I paid $2,500 for a National Football League franchise, which I named the Pirates, because the Pittsburgh baseball team was called the Pirates. It wasn't till 1940, when we held a contest for a new name, that we became the Steelers. Joe

Carr's girlfriend—Joe's been our ticket manager right along—his girlfriend won the contest. There were people who said, "That contest don't look like it was on the level."

Anyway, I bought the franchise in '33 because I figured that it would be good to have a league schedule and that eventually professional football would be good. And the reason I bought a franchise at that particular time was that we knew that Pennsylvania was going to repeal certain laws—"blue laws," they were called. You see, until then, Sunday football was illegal in Pennsylvania. This was going to be changed by the legislature. So now I had a franchise, and our schedule was made up. But a couple of days before our opening game, the mayor phoned me and said, "I got a complaint here from a preacher that this game should not be allowed because it's against the blue laws. The repeal hasn't been ratified by city council and won't be till Tuesday."

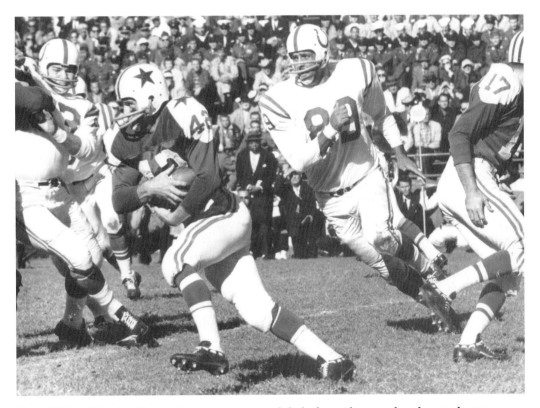

One of Gino Marchetti's greatest assets, speed, is in focus here as he chases down Dallas Cowboy Don McIlhenny in 1960. The great defensive end, playing at 6'4" and 245 pounds, defined the position during his 13-year career with the Baltimore Colts. A college teammate of Ollie Matson at San Francisco, Marchetti was named All-Pro seven times and went to 10 Pro Bowls. He entered the Pro Football Hall of Fame in 1972, the same year as did his old college teammate Matson. No. 17 is Dallas quarterback Don Meredith.

There were many adjectives used to describe the escapades of Joe Don Looney during his five-year NFL career. A powerful fullback and an accomplished punter, he was also, well, unpredictable, as most of his teammates would concur. Looney, out of Oklahoma, was drafted by the Giants in 1964 but ended up on the roster of the Colts that year, then joined the Lions for 1965 and part of 1966, then the Redskins for the other part of 1966 and 1967, and finally ended his career with the Saints in 1969.

"Well," I said, "I never heard of this thing ratification."

Nobody else had heard anything about it either, until this preacher brought it up. The mayor told me he didn't know what I could do about it but that I should go see a fellow named Harmar Denny, who was director of public safety and was over the police department.

So I went to Denny and I said, "We're in the big leagues now. We can't have a thing like this happen to our opening game." But this Denny was pretty much of a straight laced guy. All he would say was that he was going away for the weekend. "Good," I told him. "You go away." Then I went to see the superintendent of police, a man named McQuade, and told *him* my problem.

"Oh, that there's ridiculous," he said. "Give me a couple of tickets and I'll go to the game on Sunday. That'll be the last place they'll look for me if they want to stop the game."

So McQuade hid out at the game, and on the following Tuesday the council met and ratified everything. We had three thousand people at the game. Maybe thirty-five hundred.

## TURNER ON WILLIS

Chicago Bears great Bulldog Turner remembered the Browns' great 60-minute lineman Bill Willis, like Turner a Pro Football Hall of Fame honoree:

Actually, the first guy that ever convinced me that I couldn't handle anybody I ever met was Bill Willis, who played on Cleveland, and I was on my way down then. They called him the Cat. He was skinny, and he didn't look like he should be playing middle guard, but he would jump right over you. I'll tell you—the only way I could block him was I'd squat, and when he tried to jump over me, I'd come up and catch him. Every time, my nose would be right in his armpit— and later I'd tell my wife, "Goddamn, Gladys, that man perspires. I can't stand it." But that guy was a football player, and don't think he wasn't. Oh, he was a warhorse, that Willis.

Earl Morrall, out of Michigan State, quarterbacked for Pittsburgh in 1957 and 1958. During his enduring 21-year NFL career, Morrall also played for the 49ers (1956), the Lions (1958–64), the Giants (1965–67), the Colts (1968–71), and the Dolphins (1972–76).

CLEVELAND PLAIN DEALER

Chicago Bear Walter Payton had all the moves: power-plus, speed, agility, and durability. "Sweetness," as he was called, was anything but that in his encounters with would-be tacklers, the hardest-hitting back, many said, since Jim Brown. When he retired in 1987, Payton had gained more yardage in his 13-year career in Chicago than any ball carrier in NFL history (16,726), a record that would stand until Emmitt Smith exceeded it in 2002. Sweetness gained admission to the Pro Football Hall of Fame in 1993.

A bevy of Chicago Bears defenders attack San Francisco 49ers halfback Strike Strzykalski in a 1951 game. Coming over the top is versatile quarterback George Blanda, a defensive back here (he also occasionally played fullback that year for Chicago). Underneath is one of the meanest Bears ever, end Ed Sprinkle, and coming in from the left are linemen Ray Bray (No. 82) and Ed Neal (No. 58).

### LAYNE ON BINGAMAN

The great Bobby Layne recalled his teammate, the enormous Detroit Lions guard Les Bingaman:

We had Les Bingaman, who weighed about 340 pounds and was so big that when [coach] Buddy [Parker] finally retired him he told him, "I want you to quit, because I don't want you dying on the football field." Bing couldn't lose weight. He had little bitty feet—I'd say he'd wear a 9½ or a 10 shoe—and he had to tape up his arches because of that tremendous weight that he carried. But the guy was quick as a cat and a brilliant middle guard. He was captain of our team, yet he came to camp every

Y. A. Tittle, whose first name was Yelberton and whose nickname was the "Bald Eagle" (he never said which he liked least), warms up on the New York Giants sideline in the twilight of his NFL career. Tittle, out of Louisiana State University, began his 17-year NFL career with the Baltimore Colts in 1948. Three years later he joined the San Francisco 49ers, where he played 10 years (1951–60) before coming to New York to finish out the last four years. The aged Tittle led the Giants to three NFL title games during those years, but a championship eluded him in all three. The Bald Eagle was elected to the Pro Football Hall of Fame in 1971.

year with a fear of getting cut. In scrimmages he was all eyes. He looked at every-thing. He'd spot something—he'd see someone in our offense tipping off the play, and just before the snap of the ball, he'd say "Six hole!" And the defense would pile into the six hole and stop the play. I'd say, "Bing, goddamn it, tell who's tipping the play. Tell me so I can get him straightened out." But he wouldn't tell me till after training camp was over—till he'd made the team. He was all-league practically every year, but he never did stop worrying about being cut.

## BUTKUS ON ATKINS

Chicago Bears legendary linebacker Dick Butkus remembered a teammate who was equally ferocious in a game and, well, *eccentric* when the game clock wasn't running:

> Doug [Atkins, the enormous defensive end for the Bears in the fifties and sixties] owned a pit bull named Rebel. Some Saturdays, when the defensive team would meet to go over plays for the last time before home games, Doug would show up with this dead-eyed dog of his, one of the nastiest-looking creatures I've ever seen. We would meet in the locker room at Wrigley, which must have been originally designed for a two-man bowling team, and Doug would sit in the back, his legs reaching practically to the first row of desks, and next to him would be his vicious mutt.
>
> After the meetings, Doug would take Rebel out onto the field and start snapping a towel at him. Naturally, Rebel would grab the towel in his teeth, and they would play tug-of-war, each time finishing with Doug swinging the towel over his head with that idiot of a dog hanging onto the other end. After about six rotations, Doug would let go of the towel and Rebel would fly 30 to 40 yards and land with a bounce on the right-field grass. It was one of the craziest things I've ever seen.

## THE ENFORCER

In his book *Fatso*, Art Donovan, who played on the same defensive line with Baltimore Colts great Gino Marchetti, remembered the day that the great defensive end saw the light and reformed—well, at least, sort of:

> Vendettas are big in football, and just about every team has at least one enforcer, the guy whose job it is to pay for crimes, real or perceived, against your team. For his first couple of years with the Colts, Gino Marchetti was our enforcer. Gino was a tough kid from the ghetto. He went to school at Antioch College, right outside of San Francisco, and they recruited him right off the racetrack. He was a war hero whose Italian immigrant family had been interned with the northern California Japanese

Roger Staubach, scrambler extraordinaire and master of the two-minute drill, rolls out on this pass in a 1975 game against the New York Giants. His association with the "Hail Mary" pass had nothing to do with his reputation as *the* clean-cut, All-American boy, but rather with a desperation pass he tossed to Drew Pearson on a December afternoon in 1975. Staubach did, however, write an inspirational book on his life and beliefs, *Time Enough to Win*, which became a national best-seller. Pursuing him here is Giants defensive end Dave Gallagher.

Americans during the war until the local papers started running stories about all the medals Gino was winning in the Ardennes Forest. They let his folks out then.

An Antioch recruiter had spotted the big hulk at the racetrack one day and brought him along to the head coach. He immediately became a star. He could also kick some ass, and that particular talent gained him quite a reputation as not only perhaps the greatest defensive end to ever play the game but also as a dirty cheap-shot artist. Then one day Gino was born again, so to speak. He had just brought down Detroit's marvelous halfback Doak Walker, and he couldn't resist digging the heel of his hand into Walker's schnoz as he was getting up off the ground. But instead of starting a fight or yelling or anything, Walker just looked at him. Didn't say a word, just stared at Gino. Gino felt like a piece of shit.

"I could see it in his eyes," he said later. "A big guy like me, with probably 80 pounds and six inches on Walker, having to resort to a mean, low-down trick like that. That look of disgust reformed me. I'm no longer the hatchet man around here."

### JOHNNY UNITAS

Teammate Art Donovan also provided this look at one of the game's all-time greatest—if not *the* greatest—quarterbacks:

[Johnny] Unitas was always a quiet guy. Tough, but quiet. For instance, when he threw an interception he was a wild man going after the defensive man who had picked him off. And when he ran with the ball he'd inflict some major punishment, even if he did look like a wounded stork thrashing around in those black high-tops. But off the field he was as soft-spoken as a priest. My friends who played offense— guys like Raymond Berry and Jim Parker and Jim Mutscheller—they told me that this kid quarterback we picked up off the sandlots was a leader, despite his soft-spoken demeanor. In a Unitas huddle no one was allowed to talk except the quarterback, although I've heard tales that Berry never shut up in those huddles, jabbering after every play about how open he was and asking why the hell he wasn't being thrown to on every play.

[Baltimore Colts guard Alex] Sandusky tells me a story that during

Dan Reeves was a hard-charging halfback, scoring a touchdown in this 1965 game against the Pittsburgh Steelers. Reeves played for the Dallas Cowboys from 1965 to 1972. The last three of those years he also served as an assistant coach to Tom Landry. Reeves got his first head coaching job in 1981 when he took over at Denver, where he would lead the Broncos for the next 12 years, taking them to three Super Bowls (XXI, XXII, and XXIV) but never winning one. He coached the New York Giants (1993–96) and then took over the Atlanta Falcons (1997–2003), taking them to Super Bowl XXXIII, but lost to his old Denver team.

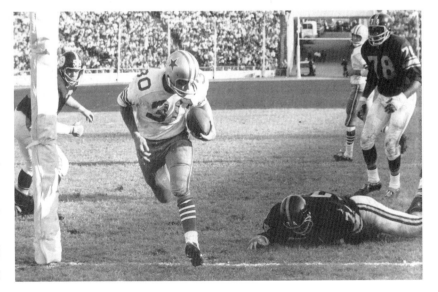

the 49ers game in 1958 here in Baltimore, Unitas kept calling Lenny Moore's number in the huddle, and Moore kept slashing through the San Francisco defense. So after about half a dozen straight runs by Moore, Lenny came back to the huddle and told John, "Hey, man, cool it. I'm getting tired."

Whooaa. Nobody tells John Unitas to "cool it." Unitas' face turned into a flinty stare, and his eyeballs nearly burned a hole through Lenny's head. "Listen, asshole, nobody tells me to cool it," Unitas said. "I'll run your ass till you die."

He put the fear of God into him, and by this time Lenny's stammering, "Forget it, John. Forget I said anything. Give me the ball, please. Give me the ball on every play."

### LOONEY, AS IN JOE DON

Frank Gifford talked about Joe Don Looney, the Giants' first-round draft choice for 1964, who had a personality all his own:

He had the potential to be an extraordinary player. But . . . there were problems. He injured his leg early in training camp. So [coach Allie] Sherman told him to see the trainer about it. To Allie's amazement, Looney refused.

His reason? "It's my leg. I know more about it than the trainer."

He wouldn't go to Detroit for an exhibition game. "I can't play; why should I go?" he asked me.

"You're part of the team," I said.

"I'm not part of the team if I can't play," he replied.

Joe Don came in an hour after curfew one night and was fined. "Not fair," he said. "I was in bed an hour early last night, so we should even up."

He wouldn't throw his used socks into a marked bin because "I'm not going to do what any sign tells me to do."

Although I didn't see it, I understand that in scrimmages he often ran one way when a play called for him to go another. His reason: "Anybody can run where the blockers are. A good football player makes his own holes."

As a last-ditch measure, [Giants owner] Wellington Mara and Allie Sherman asked Y. A. [Tittle] and me to try to talk to the young man. Joe Don was 6'1", 224 pounds, and ran the hundred in something like 9.7. They wanted to keep him.

We were still in training camp at Fairfield University. Joe Don was lying down in his room listening to music when we found him.

Y.A. flopped on the other bed and started to tell Joe Don about his trade to New York from San Francisco, which somehow Y.A. equated with Looney's problems—

how difficult it was leaving the team where he had spent most of his career, his family, his business; being traded for a rookie lineman; coming to a team in a strange city with a popular quarterback [Charlie Conerly] ahead of him; and how "alone" Y.A. had felt.

Clearly talking from his heart and, perhaps, for the first time outside of his family, discussing his gut feeling about the trade, Tittle went on for about 20 minutes with Joe Don and me listening intently.

Finally Y.A. finished and stopped—serious, sad, thinking of what had happened just three years earlier.

Joe Don broke an embarrassing silence. He sat up, completely caught up in Tittle's reverie, and said sympathetically, "It must have been really tough, Y.A. Anything I can do for you?"

Tittle's counsel apparently went for naught because Looney was traded to the Colts before the first game of the 1964 regular season.

## PRAGMATISM PREVAILS

Things are not always as they appear; so reports author Abby Mendelson in his history of the Pittsburgh Steelers:

There is no more touching tableau in the Steelers' rich history than that of Joe Greene carrying stricken comrade Lynn Swann off the field in the 1975 AFC Championship Game.

Swann, who took his fair share of abuse as the Steelers' wide receiver of choice in the seventies, had been knocked cold and was lying supine on the Three Rivers Stadium turf.

Before play could be stopped, Greene ran out and picked up Swann. It was a heart-rending scene, and there wasn't a dry eye in the house.

"People always talk about that," Swann says, "saying that Joe must have cared about me a great deal. Joe didn't care about me that much," Swann shakes his head. "He just didn't want to waste a timeout. Joe was always trying to figure out how to win a ballgame."

## CEMENT HEAD

The last NFL player to go helmetless was about what you'd expect. On the field, Chicago Bears end Dick Plasman was ferocious, tough, and mean. Away from it, he was a loner who could do crazy things "with booze, with girls, and so forth. Not the kinds of things you'd want to put in your book," a teammate said.

Plasman's bareheaded career lasted from 1937 to 1941. He then went into the service for two years, and during that time the NFL made the headgear mandatory (beginning in 1943). He wore a helmet in his last three seasons—one with the Bears, two with the Cardinals.

Plasman said he simply wasn't comfortable in a helmet. He hadn't used one in high school or college (Vanderbilt) and didn't see any reason to change once he got to the pros. He was 6'3", about 225, and could more than take care of himself. He grew his hair long and thick to provide some padding against blows, but teammates said he probably didn't need it.

"About the only way you could have taken advantage of it was with a baseball bat," said back Hugh Gallarneau. "I mean, he had a piece of cement for a head."

## OLD QUARTERBACKS NEVER DIE

There's never been an unlikelier MVP than George Blanda in 1970. He was the oldest player in the league, a 43-year-old kicker and backup quarterback. But during one sensational five-week stretch he became a national story as he kicked and passed the Oakland Raiders to four victories and a tie.

Without his heroics, the team wouldn't have finished first in the AFC West. How did George do it?

October 25 vs. Pittsburgh: replaced injured Daryle Lamonica in the first quarter and threw three touchdown passes (44, 19, and 43 yards) to lead the Raiders to a 31–14 win.

November 1 at Kansas City: booted a 48-yard field goal with three seconds left to salvage a 17–17 tie. The Chiefs had 6'10" Morris Stroud stand by the goal post and try to bat the ball down, but it just cleared his fingertips—and the crossbar.

November 8 vs. Cleveland: came in to quarterback in the fourth quarter after Lamonica got hurt again. Hit Warren Wells with a 14-yard touchdown pass to tie the game at 20 with 1:14 remaining, then kicked a 52-yard field goal, his longest as a Raider, with three seconds to go for the victory. Blanda: "I didn't kick it any different than last week. Well, maybe I put a little more rear end into it." *San Francisco Chronicle* headline: "It's Blanda Again!"

November 15 at Denver: took over for Lamonica with 4:01 to play and the Broncos leading, 19–17. Drove the team 80 yards on four completions, the last a 20-yarder to Fred Biletnikoff for the winning score. Headline: "Routine Raider Win—Blanda Again."

November 22 vs. San Diego: booted a 16-yard field goal with four seconds left for a 20–17 victory. Had missed earlier tries from 42 and 41 yards. Blanda: "Hell, I was just setting up those last few seconds." Headline: "Ho-Hum, Blanda Again."

Blanda's run finally ended on Thanksgiving Day against the Lions in Detroit. He was put in in the fourth quarter but couldn't produce any points as the Raiders lost, 28–14.

### IRWIN SHAW ON Y. A. TITTLE

The renowned author of *The Young Lions* (not Detroit's) and other literary works was also a New York Giants football fan. He especially remembered Y. A. Tittle in an article he wrote for *Esquire* magazine in 1965:

> He almost always seems to be in desperate trouble, and almost always seems to get out of it at the last fateful moment. Whether the record bears it out or not, the Giants always seem to be behind, and in the good days, at least, Tittle put them ahead when all hope seemed lost. It's the Alamo every Sunday, with Davy Crockett sighting down his long rifle with the powder running out, and Jim Bowie asking to be carried across the line with his knife in his hand.

### ON STAUBACH

Dallas Cowboys quarterback Roger Staubach, besides earning a place in both the College and the Pro Football Halls of Fame, also had the reputation of being one of the game's most clean-cut heroes. Some contemporaries commented on that:

> "We're going to have to do something about this guy. He's going to ruin the image of an NFL quarterback if he doesn't start smoking, drinking, cussing, or something."
>
> —Don Meredith

> "There's no question in my mind that when he finished playing he was the number one sports hero in the United States. I think he crossed all age barriers, he crossed everything. He was what people wanted to see when they thought of an authentic American hero. That's who they wanted to see—Roger Staubach. That rubs off a helluva lot on the organization."
>
> —Tex Schramm

> "His idea of breaking training is putting whipped cream on his pie."
>
> —Bob St. John, Dallas *Morning News*

> "He can play until he's 40 because he doesn't know what a hangover is."
>
> —Sonny Jurgensen

Baltimore's Jim O'Brien (No. 80) celebrates the game-winning field goal he had just kicked to defeat the Dallas Cowboys in Super Bowl V in Miami on January 17, 1971.

**7**

## The Ultimate Game

"If it's the ultimate game, how come they're playing it again next year?"

—DALLAS COWBOYS RUNNING BACK DUANE THOMAS

AT SUPER BOWL VI

The Super Bowl, today an institution in the world of American sports much the same as major league baseball's World Series, came about as a result of the merger of the National Football League and the first league to successfully challenge it, the American Football League, which was founded in 1959 by Lamar Hunt and began regular-season play the following year.

All earlier challengers, like the three that also bore the AFL name and the All-America Football Conference, which emerged after World War II, had failed. But Hunt's league was destined not only to survive but to thrive, bringing professional football to fans in areas where it had not existed before and enticing players of the highest quality to join its ranks.

The competition for players—the salary war, as it was known—as well as the struggle for equal recognition between the two leagues went on for six years. Early in 1966, however, secret meetings were held between Hunt and Tex Schramm of the Dallas Cowboys regarding a merger of the two leagues. They forged a plan and, on June 8 of that year, NFL Commissioner Pete Rozelle announced that the two bastions of professional football in the United States would indeed merge into a single, expanded league. Part of the plan was to stage a championship game between the prevailing teams in each of the two leagues, the first scheduled for January 1967. That first championship game, played between the Packers and the Chiefs at the Los Angeles Memorial Coliseum, did not have the title "Super Bowl," nor was it even a sellout, with just over sixty-three thousand fans in attendance. But all that was about to change.

The following year, the championship game became quasi-officially known as the Super Bowl, the name attributed to Lamar Hunt although it was the press and the media who, with great zest, jumped on it and inscribed it forever as pro football's annual superlative moment.

The senior league representatives, Vince Lombardi's Packers, easily dominated the first two years, but then came the New York Jets and their brash quarterback Joe Namath to prove that the NFL (the two leagues did not become conferences until 1970) did not have a lock on the championship. Since then there have been teams besides the Packers to win multiple times: the Dolphins, Steelers, Cowboys, Raiders, 49ers, Redskins, Giants, and Broncos; and, of course, a pair of multiple also-rans: the Vikings and the Bills. It has showcased great talent and fervid competition.

Over the years, the Super Bowl has become the quintessential Sunday of the professional football season. Hype is its middle name; extravaganza is its essence. Hundreds of millions watch it on television in the United States and countries throughout the world. It has truly become a sports classic.

**Green Bay Packers quarterback Bart Starr passes in Super Bowl I. He was 16 of 23 for 211 yards and two touchdowns that day, as Vince Lombardi's Pack destroyed Hank Stram's Kansas City Chiefs, 35–10. The game was designated the AFL-NFL World Championship Game that year, not getting "Super Bowl" designation until the following year. It was played at the Los Angeles Coliseum.**

## THE NAME!

Who came up with the name Super Bowl?

American Football League founder Lamar Hunt. Also the owner of the Dallas Texans (later the Kansas City Chiefs), Hunt told how he stumbled on the term:

American
Football League
founder Lamar
Hunt came up
with the name
*Super Bowl.*

> My kids have this ball; maybe you've seen it advertised on television. It's about the
> size of a handball, but it bounces 10 times higher than a normal ball. They call it a
> Super Ball. My kids kept talking about it so much that the name stuck in my mind. It
> just popped out—Super Bowl—when we started meetings to arrange the champi-
> onship game [between the NFL and the AFL in the mid-sixties].

## SUPER BOWL EVE

The first and only time the Chicago Bears went to the Super Bowl was at the end of the 1985 season (Super Bowl XX). Mike Ditka was the coach—at the time only the third person ever to go to the classic as both a player (as a Cowboy at Super Bowl VI) and a coach (the other two: Tom Flores and Forrest Gregg)—and the

Green Bay's Max McGee (No. 85) takes off here as Paul Hornung sets to launch a pass to him in a game against the New York Giants. McGee, an elder statesman in football terms by Super Bowl I, had the greatest game of his career that day, catching seven passes for 138 yards, two of them for touchdowns. Hornung did not play in Super Bowl I because of an injury.

**Commissioner Pete Rozelle presents the winning trophy to Green Bay Packers coach Vince Lombardi following Super Bowl I.**

Oakland Raiders running back Hewitt Dixon finds a big hole in the Packers line, something that did not occur ofter during Super Bowl II. Behind him is Raiders quarterback Daryle Lamonica. The two Packers aiming to close the hole are linebacker Dave Robinson (No. 89) and safety Tom Brown (No. 40).

Joe Namath hands the ball off to Matt Snell in the Jets' victory over the Colts in Super Bowl III in Miami.

"No other single American event impacts the sale of avocados like the Super Bowl."

—MARK AFFLECK, CALIFORNIA AVOCADO COMMISSION PRESIDENT

lineup included such memorable stars as Walter Payton, Mike Singletary, Jim McMahon, and Dan Hampton.

Hampton, one of the game's great defensive linemen and Pro Football Hall of Fame inductee in 2002, had this special memory of the thrill of it all:

> All that season I used to ride with Ming [fellow defensive lineman Steve McMichael] to practice, and every day we'd talk about going to the Super Bowl, how great it would be. And then, after the last playoff game, we got in the car and looked at each other, and we said, "We can finally say we're going." It was a very moving moment.
>
> I remember especially the night before the Super Bowl. It was kind of an emotional thing; we'd been ready for so long. We had meetings that night. In ours, the defense, we were going to watch a game film, and by this time we were sick of films. As I was going in there, I said, "Hey, Ming, I cannot watch another roll of film. We got to do something."
>
> I'm watching about the sixth play, and my heart's beating fast, I can't wait, so I just got up and kicked the projector off the little table it was sitting on. Ming, at that moment, leaped up and grabbed a chair and screamed some expletive about the Patriots and swung the chair at the chalkboard that had all these plays diagrammed on it. All four legs stuck into the chalkboard. Nobody said anything, and finally I just said, "Let's get the hell out of here." We all walked out of the room, no one saying anything, and went to our rooms and went to sleep. And everybody knows what happened the next day [the Bears won 46–10, then the largest margin of victory in Super Bowl history].

## EXECUTIVE PRIVILEGE

Former President Gerald Ford watched Super Bowl XIII, between the Pittsburgh Steelers and the Dallas Cowboys, while on a trip to Israel. President Ronald Reagan tossed the coin at the White House prior to Super Bowl XIX, between the San Francisco 49ers and the Miami Dolphins, and his performance was shown via television on the scoreboard at Stanford Stadium. President George H. W. Bush made a taped message for the U.S. military forces engaged in Desert Storm, and it was shown on television at halftime of Super Bowl XXV, between the New York Giants and the Buffalo Bills.

Mr. Bush, as vice president, attended Super Bowl XVI, between the 49ers and the Cincinnati Bengals, at the Pontiac Silverdome. He is the highest-ranking United States official to attend a Super Bowl.

**Chiefs coach Hank Stram consults with quarterback Len Dawson during Super Bowl IV in New Orleans. Kansas City defeated the Minnesota Vikings 23–7.**

### HOLY GUACAMOLE

According to Mark Affleck, California Avocado Commission President:

> **No other single American event impacts the sale of avocados like the Super Bowl. In fact, Super Bowl week trails only *Cinco de Mayo* as the most important week of the year for California avocados.**

Affleck made this comment as he announced guacamole recipes named in honor of Super Bowl contenders.

### DOCTOR'S ORDERS

Unable to obtain a hotel room for Super Bowl XII— Cowboys vs. Broncos—in New Orleans, a healthy and wealthy Texan had a physician friend check him into one of that city's finest hospitals (a reasonable $100 per day in 1978) for unconfining "observation." Dallas remedied his "ills" with a 27–10 victory over Denver.

### SPACED OUT

The NFL and NASA have more in common than acronyms. A number of astronauts have been involved with Super Bowl games.

*Apollo 8* astronauts Frank Borman, James Lovell, and William Anders, fresh from lunar orbit, led the crowd in the Pledge of Allegiance at Super Bowl III. The *Apollo 17* crew of Eugene Cernan, Ronald Evans, and Harrison Schmitt led the Pledge of Allegiance at Super Bowl VII.

Giving added dimension to the term "live via satellite," the crew of *Skylab 3*—Alan Bean, Jack Lousma, and Owen Garriott—watched Super Bowl VIII from Earth orbit during its mission.

At Super Bowl XXIII in Miami, a tribute to NASA and the Kennedy Space Center was part of the pregame show. Eight astronauts representing four phases of America's space program—Mercury, Gemini, Apollo, and the space shuttle— appeared along with space vehicles such as a lunar rover and hardware supplied by the Space and Rocket Center at

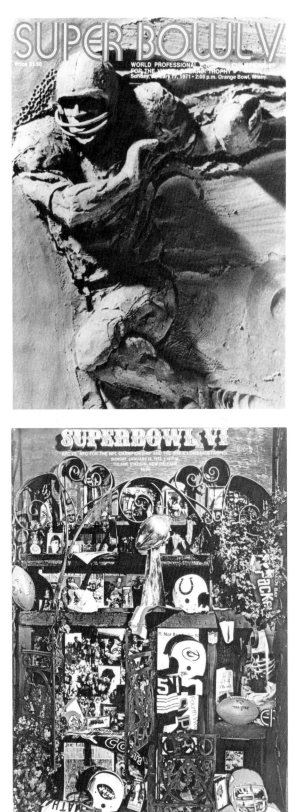

Roger Staubach scrambles out of the pocket in Dallas' 24–3 victory over Miami in Super Bowl VI in New Orleans.

**Friendly rivals:** Miami head coach Don Shula (left) and Washington Redskins head coach George Allen at a Washington Touchdown Club luncheon after Super Bowl VII. Shula had a lot to smile about: his Dolphins triumphed 14–7 in the title game as they became the first and only team ever to go through the NFL regular and postseasons undefeated (17–0–0). Allen, ever the supreme optimist, was undoubtedly smiling about the next season to come.

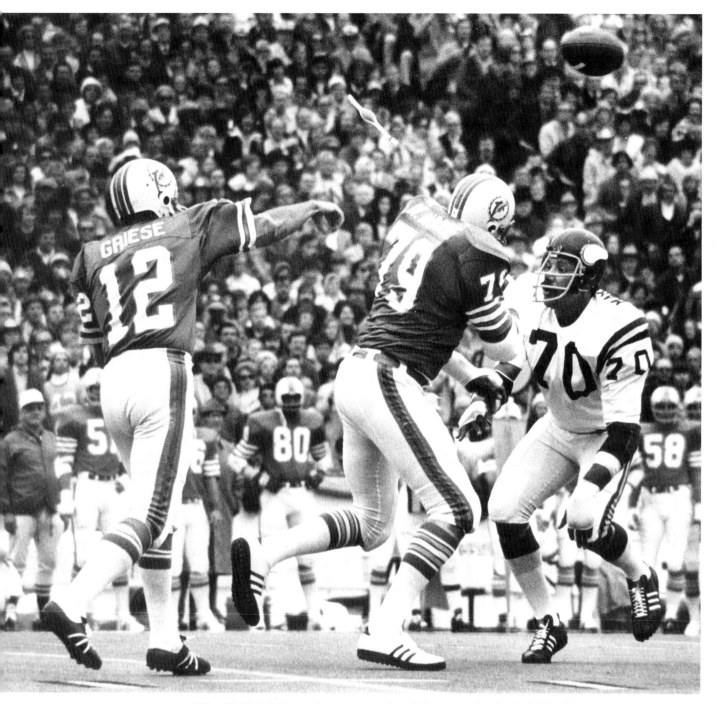

**Miami's Bob Griese airs it out against Minnesota in the Dolphins' Super Bowl VIII victory in Houston.**

**Minnesota's Alan Page (No. 88) closes in on Pittsburgh's Franco Harris during the
Steelers' 16–7 victory in Super Bowl IX in New Orleans.**

**Pittsburgh's Dwight White brings down Cowboys quarterback Roger Staubach in Super Bowl X, won 21–17 by the Steelers.**

Huntsville, Alabama. At Super Bowl XXIII were Gordon Cooper, Dick Gordon, Pete Conrad, and the crew of space shuttle *Atlantis*—Robert "Hoot" Gibson, Guy Gardner, Mike Mullane, Jerry Ross, and William Shepard.

## VIEW FROM THE QUARTERBACK

Phil Simms quarterbacked the New York Giants to their first Super Bowl appearance after the 1986 season. Bill Parcells was his coach, and his teammates included such luminaries as Lawrence Taylor, Joe Morris, Jim Burt, and Mark Bavaro. Played at the Rose Bowl in Pasadena, California, Super Bowl XXI was to be Simms' day of destiny, but it took a while before that game's Most Valuable Player would realize it. As he recalled:

> I remember going into the locker room at halftime out there, with us losing 10–9. I was thinking, well, hell, everything we're trying to do is working. How come we're not ahead? Still, I wasn't concerned; being down didn't seem something significant to me at the time. It was just a matter of making a few plays click, I kept saying to myself, and we'll score every time we get the ball. And it happened. In the second half we made a couple of big plays and scored, got on top, and then the defense just totally shut down the Broncos.

Oakland's Ken Stabler drops back to pass in the Raiders' 32–14 win over Minnesota in Super Bowl XI.

Raiders coach John Madden gets a lift from his players after winning Super Bowl XI on January 9, 1977, in Pasadena, California.

**Denver actually made it work out well for me. They were determined not to get beat by letting us run the ball, which opened up the passing game to us. We took advantage of that.**

That they did. Simms completed 22 of 25 passes for 268 yards, including 3 touchdown passes, as the Giants beat the Broncos 39–20.

### THE FANS—1993

Various studies at recent Super Bowls indicate the following demographics among attending fans:

- Median age of 41
- 81 percent male
- 68 percent attending first or second Super Bowl
- 5 percent from foreign countries
- 11 percent accompanied by child under age 17
- 33 percent with income greater than $100,000
- 75 percent with income greater than $70,000
- 27 percent business owners
- 25 percent corporate officers

### A MOSAIC

According to Marshall McLuhan, educator and philosopher:

**The Super Bowl is a world theater. The world is a happening. In the speedup of the electronic age, we want things to happen. This offers us a mosaic that the fans love—everything is in action at once.**

### A MAN FOR ALL DECADES

Only one player, Gene Upshaw, has played in Super Bowls in three different decades. Upshaw, who was inducted into the Pro Football Hall of Fame in 1987, played guard for the Oakland Raiders from 1967 to 1981 and participated with the AFL/AFC champions in Super Bowls II (1968), XI (1977), and XV (1981).

One other player, Jeff Rutledge, was a Super Bowl participant in two different decades, but also was a member of a team

**Eagles quarterback Ron Jaworski sidesteps Oakland's Mike Davis during the Raiders' 27–10 win in Super Bowl XV.**

that was the NFC champion in a third decade. Rutledge was on the roster of the 1979 Los Angeles Rams, who played in Super Bowl XIV (1980), and he played for the New York Giants in Super Bowl XXI (1987) and the Washington Redskins in Super Bowl XXVI (1992).

### MATT'S THE ONE

Linebacker Matt Millen, who retired following the 1991 season, is the only player to earn Super Bowl championship rings with three different teams: the Raiders in Super Bowls XV and XVIII, the 49ers in Super Bowl XXIV, and the Redskins in Super Bowl XXVI.

### LOMBARDI TROPHY

The Vince Lombardi Trophy is presented each year to the winner of the Super Bowl for permanent possession.

It is a memorial to the late coach of the Green Bay Packers, who won Super Bowls I and II and NFL championships in 1961, 1962, and 1965. Following four years as the AFL-NFL World Championship Game Trophy, it was renamed for Lombardi in 1970.

The Lombardi Trophy is handcrafted of sterling silver—including nuts and bolts—stands 21 inches high, and weighs seven pounds, three ounces. A stylized football of regulation size sits atop a three-sided base with convex faces. Each trophy is valued at $10,000 and is crafted by Tiffany & Co.

### TOUGH TALK

In the days before Super Bowl I, which pitted Vince Lombardi's Green Bay Packers against Hank Stram's Kansas City Chiefs, the tradition of trash talk in the week preceding the classic-to-be was launched, and the person who gets the credit is Chiefs defensive back Fred Williamson. The story of the creation of that less-than-auspicious tradition was told by author Lou Sahadi in *Super Sundays I-XIV*:

**The tranquility of the Chiefs training grounds was disrupted a few days after the players were getting settled in their West Coast environs [the game was being played at the Coliseum in Los Angeles]. Fred Williamson, their controversial cornerback,**

Chicago Bears defensive tackle-turned-fullback William "Refrigerator" Perry plows in for a touchdown in Super Bowl XX. The Bears annihilated the New England Patriots that day at the Louisiana Superdome in New Orleans, 46–10, then the largest margin of victory in Super Bowl history.

Bears quarterback Jim McMahon (No. 9) dives in for a touchdown in Super Bowl XX.

Chicago Bears head coach Mike Ditka after Super Bowl XX, posing with the coveted Vince Lombardi Trophy, awarded to the winner of each year's Super Bowl.

**Phil Simms passes his way to a record-setting performance against Denver in Super Bowl XXI, a 39–20 Giants victory in Pasadena.**

Denver Broncos quarterback John Elway (No. 7) confronts the defensive rush of Washington Redskins tackle Dexter Manley (No. 72) in Super Bowl XXII. The Skins could do no wrong that day; behind the superb quarterbacking of Doug Williams and the awesome defense led by Manley, they demolished the Broncos at Jack Murphy Stadium in San Diego, 42–10.

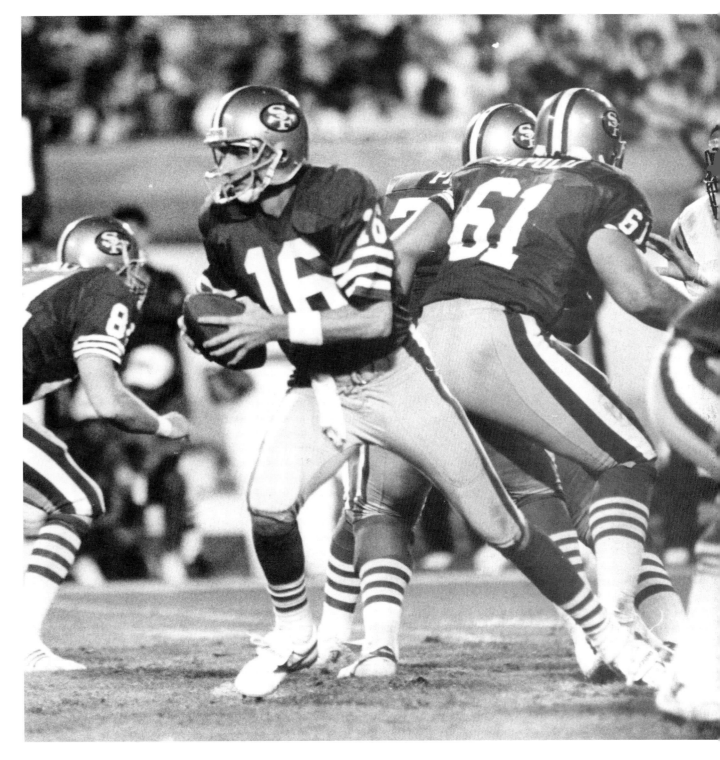

**San Francisco's Joe Montana drops back to pass in the 49ers' last-minute, 20–16 win over Cincinnati in Super Bowl XXIII.**

**The 49ers set the tone early in Super Bowl XXIV in New Orleans, leaving little doubt by the time the clock wound down.**

was making inflammatory statements about the Packers in general and some players in particular. Williamson himself had been a subject of discussion throughout the season for his rough style of play. He was a vicious tackler who would come around with his right arm, fist clenched, taking aim at his opponent's head while making a tackle. Because of the maneuver, he was known as the "Hammer."

"I haven't seen anything in the films that offers much of a threat to me," boasted Williamson. "I'll be able to cover either Boyd Dowler or Carroll Dale. I don't see any Lance Alworths, Charlie Hennigans, or Elbert Dubenions in their films. Dale and Dowler don't have the speed or the combination moves of our own Otis Taylor.... I guarantee you they won't beat me on a deep pattern.... I'll just dump Dowler when he leaves the line of scrimmage. If he catches the ball, I'll drop the hammer on him. Two hammers on Dowler and one on Dale should be enough. Bart Starr? Who's he, anyway?"

Well, Starr was the guy who completed 16 of 23 passes for 250 yards, including two touchdowns, to help the Packers beat the Chiefs 35–10.

## STARBUCK AND STAUBACH

In his autobiography *It's Only a Game*, Pittsburgh quarterback Terry Bradshaw recalls this incident after the Steelers had won Super Bowl X in 1976:

I was invited to the White House to meet President Gerald Ford and Vice President Nelson Rockefeller. This was a great thrill for me; I had literally gone from the outhouse to the White House. I invited my future second ex-wife-to-be, Olympic figure skater Jo Jo Starbuck, to go with me. Man, I was feeling mighty proud of myself; I was the quarterback of the Super Bowl champions, my 64-yard touchdown pass to Lynn

Pete Rozelle (right) holds the Super Bowl MVP award, named in his honor, prior to Super Bowl XXV, while NFL commissioner Paul Tagliabue handles the time-honored Lombardi Trophy, awarded to each year's Super Bowl Champion.

Swann had won the game, I was dating a beautiful and famous skater, my picture was on the cover of newspapers and magazines around the country. I had made it.

During the party following a show starring Carol Burnett, Jo Jo Starbuck and I were introduced to Vice President Rockefeller. This was most definitely the first time the names Bradshaw and Rockefeller had ever been used in the same sentence. The vice president was very kind to me. "You know, fella," he said, "you're the best quarterback I've ever seen . . ."

Wow!

". . . I've always enjoyed watching how cool you are under pressure . . ."

Ah, shucks.

". . . and you're definitely a role model to the young people of this country."

Hope you're listening to this, Jo Jo.

"Why, from that first game I saw you play at the Naval Academy . . ."

Uh-oh.

". . . and when the Cowboys drafted you I thought . . ."

Obviously, the vice president had heard the name Starbuck and decided I was Roger Staubach, the Dallas Cowboys quarterback, who had *not* won Super Bowl X.

**Green Bay's Leroy Butler brings down Patriots quarterback Drew Bledsoe during the Packers' 35–21 Super Bowl XXXI win in New Orleans.**

## THE PRESIDENT HERE

As tradition now has it, the president of the United States treats the Super Bowl with the same regard as a coronation or the death of a head of state. And when its outcome has been determined, he is on the telephone to the victors. President Ronald Reagan was no exception.

When he finally got through to coach Joe Gibbs in the victorious Redskins' locker room after Super Bowl XVII, he told Gibbs: "Last week I was thinking of asking John Riggins to change the spelling of his name, add an *e* and an *a* to it. Now I'm thinking of asking him if he'd mind if I changed the spelling of my name to put *i* and another *g* in it."

After hearing that, Riggins said: "Ron is the president, but I'm the king." After a pause: "At least for tonight." After another pause: "Aw, I was just joking."

## SHOW TIME

The Super Bowl has never been known for understatement or its lack of conspicuous consumption, pizzazz, hype, and pageantry, much less for a shortage of celebrities. As Ira Berkow wrote for *The New York Times* regarding Super Bowl XVIII:

> **Not since 1539, when Hernando de Soto arrived with the greatest sea armada ever assembled for the New World exploration, has Tampa Bay experienced anything like Super Bowl week.**
>
> **An estimated 80,000 people, pachyderms, and football players trooped in to participate in the numerous events of the week, many of which were conceived in the small banner-strewn downtown section of this town of about 300,000.**
>
> **Frank Sinatra crooned, Jesse Jackson orated, Bob Hope joked, and belly dancers gyrated.**
>
> **Jane Fonda was here, Ted Koppel was here, but a former college lineman, Ronald Reagan was a no-show. He was receiving the "leather-helmet" award at the National Football League alumni dinner Saturday night but called in his regrets and appreciation.**

Why were they all there, or almost all? Because it was, in the vernacular of Sid Caesar, the show of all shows. It lasts a week until Super Bowl Sunday finally dawns. And even then, the show still goes on: before, in, and around the game itself. This excerpt from the official program of Super Bowl XVIII gives an idea of the last act of the show—the Super Sunday crescendo:

"Ron is the president, but I'm the king. . . . Aw, I was just joking."

—SUPER BOWL XVII MVP
JOHN RIGGINS

**The Rams and the Titans lined up against one another in Atlanta for Super Bowl XXXIV, a game that went down to the final play before St. Louis could claim victory.**

## SPECTACULARS

Super Bowl XVIII pregame festivities will begin at Tampa Stadium 90 minutes before kickoff with highlights of the past 17 Super Bowls, which will be shown on the Diamond Vision scoreboard. . . .

One of the world's most popular recording artists, Barry Manilow, will be singing the National Anthem today. Manilow has an incredible string of 25 consecutive "Top 40" hits and 10 straight platinum albums (given for sales of one to four million). To date, he has total international sales of 50 million records. Manilow, who has won an Emmy, Grammy, and has been voted the American Music Award's Top Male Pop Vocalist, also has been selected the United Way of America's National Chairman for Youth and Voluntarism.

During the National Anthem, a color guard from MacDill Air Force Base near Tampa will be stationed on the field. As the anthem is being played, a huge (160' x 97') American flag donated by Thomas (Ski) Demski will be unfurled. The flag will stretch from the goal line to the 50-yard line.

One of the NFL's most famous figures, Bronko Nagurski, will be today's honorary coin tosser prior to kickoff. The legendary Chicago Bears fullback (who played with the Bears from 1930 to 1937 and in 1943) was elected as a charter member of the Pro Football Hall of Fame in 1963.

Walt Disney World in Orlando, Florida, promises the Super Bowl's most spectacular halftime show yet, which is titled "Super Bowl XVIII's Salute to the Superstars of the Silver Screen."

The show will feature all of the favorite Disney characters, as well as 1,200–1,400 other performers, the bulk of whom are made up of local students from Hillsborough School District in Tampa.

Disney held auditions in October at local schools and any interested student in the district was encouraged to participate. The students who were selected began group rehearsals at 11 area high schools late in December. The individual groups rehearsed three to four times in a three-week period, and last Sunday, Disney brought the groups together for a walk-through practice. On Friday, January 20, a full-scale dress rehearsal was held at Tampa's Laito High School.

Getting all the various elements and performers to the game will be a challenge for Walt Disney World. A platoon of 50–60 buses will be used to transport the performers to Tampa Stadium. The buses will arrive after kickoff in an attempt to avoid the traffic prior to the game. After the buses have arrived, all the performers will assemble outside the stadium and wait for halftime to begin. During the show, a stage crew of 200 will be on hand to help facilitate set changes.

## HUDDLE TO SIDELINE

Tom Flores was the first person to earn Super Bowl rings as a player, assistant coach, and head coach. He was a backup quarterback for the Kansas City Chiefs in Super Bowl IV and an assistant for the Oakland Raiders in Super Bowl XI. And as a head coach he led the Oakland Raiders to victory in Super Bowl XV and coached the winning Los Angeles Raiders in Super Bowl XVIII.

## MOTORMOUTH

Dallas linebacker Thomas "Hollywood" Henderson was never at a loss for words, as he amply demonstrated before Super Bowl XIII, in which the Cowboys were to face the Pittsburgh Steelers. As he explained:

> When my mouth is running, my motor is running. If I was mute, I couldn't play this game. I put a lot of pressure on myself to see if I can play up to my mouth. . . .
>
> The Steelers do have class, but they lack depth. That's their problem. . . . Look at their tight end Randy Grossman. He's a substitute. . . . He's the smallest guy I ever played against. I've handled Russ Francis and Riley Odoms, just to name a few. . . .
>
> I'll tell you they have a real intimidating defense. They're the Pittsburgh Killers. I think the best thing for our defense to do this week is pull out the acetylene equipment, welding gear, and go into the steel mill and disrupt it. I took welding. I know all about metals and steel. They got the Steel Curtain and we got the Great Wall of China. . . . I think it will be a defensive struggle, but we will prevail.

Wrong on both counts—the Steelers won 35–31.

"When my mouth is running, my motor is running . . . . I put a lot of pressure on myself to see if I can play up to my mouth. . . ."

—DALLAS LINEBACKER THOMAS "HOLLYWOOD" HENDERSON

# AFTERWORD

I came to the National Football League in 1957, before the sport was the big business it is today—when it was a game you played because you flat-out loved it.

I was the bonus choice of the 1957 NFL draft (the first player selected), picked by the Packers, who were coming off a last-place, 4–8 season. But they didn't know what to do with me. Our coach during my first year, Lisle Blackbourn, tried me at quarterback, at halfback, at fullback, and all but gave up on me. The following year it was the same thing with Scooter McLean, who had replaced Blackbourn.

Those were two truly frustrating—not to mention losing—seasons, and included the single worst record in Green Bay history (1–10–1, in 1958). I was ready to quit pro football altogether and go back home to Kentucky. I didn't need the Packers, and they didn't seem to need me. I didn't want to be playing up there with a bunch of guys who didn't give a crap.

Then, in 1959, Vince Lombardi came to Green Bay. It was a turning point in my life and certainly in the Packers' story—and the NFL's, for that matter.

Lombardi got our attention immediately. From day one at Green Bay, we learned that things would never be the same. He told us if we didn't give him 100 percent all the time, our butts would be out of Green Bay. He laid down his rules right away.

That's what all of us needed. That's what I needed. From high school through college, I had coaches who bitched at me. That never bothered me. Lombardi bitched at everyone. He was tough—tougher than any coach I had ever known. But when he talked to us, he was direct and firm, and I started to want to play the game again.

He told me that I was going to be his halfback—not quarterback or fullback, but halfback. I had one position to focus on, and I was determined to make the best of it.

For eight years Vince Lombardi was the most important man in my life. I respected him as a coach, a leader, and, more importantly, as a friend. If I needed advice, I could talk to him. He was tougher on me than he was on most of the other players, but I needed that extra push.

It was a wonderful ride, those years that followed. The first year under Lombardi we went from having won only one game the year before to a 7–5–0 record. The next year we went to the NFL championship game, but lost to the Eagles. Then we took the NFL title two years in a row. We won another world championship in 1965, and the following year still another when we beat Kansas City in Super Bowl I.

It was a time in my life that I will treasure forever.

—**Paul Hornung**

# BIBLIOGRAPHY

Bisheff, Steve. *Los Angeles Rams*. Rutledge Books, New York: MacMillan Publishing Co., 1973.

Blair, Sam. *Dallas Cowboys, Pro or Con?* Garden City, New York: Doubleday, 1970.

Bradshaw, Terry, with David Fisher. *It's Only a Game*. New York: Pocket Books, 2001.

Butkus, Dick, with Pat Smith. *Flesh and Blood*. New York: Doubleday, 1997.

Cameron, Steve. *The Packers!* Dallas: Taylor Publishing Co., 1993.

Clary, Jack. *Pro Football's Great Moments*. New York: Bonanza Books, 1983.

Cope, Myron. *The Game That Was*. Cleveland: World Publishing Co., 1970.

Curran, Bob. *Pro Football's Rag Days*. New York: Bonanza Books, 1969.

Daly, Dan, and Bob O'Donnell. *The Pro Football Chronicle*. New York: Macmillan Publishing Co., 1990.

Donovan, Arthur J., and Bob Drury. *Fatso*. New York: Wm. Morrow & Co., 1987.

Eskenazi, Gerald. *There Were Giants in Those Days*. New York: Grossett & Dunlap, 1976.

Golenbock, Peter. *Cowboys Have Always Been My Heroes*. New York: Warner Books, 1997.

Grange, Red, with Ira Morton. *The Red Grange Story*. Urbana, Illinois: University of Illinois Press, 1993.

Griffith, Corinne. *My Life with the Redskins*. New York: A. S. Barnes & Co., 1947.

Halas, George, with Gwen Morgan and Arthur Veysey. *Halas by Halas*. New York: McGraw-Hill, 1979.

Klobuchar, Jim. *Purple Hearts and Golden Memories*. Coal Valley, Illinois: Quality Sports Publications, 1995.

Kramer, Jerry, and Dick Schaap. *Instant Replay*. Cleveland: World Publishing Co., 1968.

Liebman, Glenn. *Sports Shorts*. Chicago: Contemporary Books, 1993.

*Lions Pride*. Dallas: Taylor Publishing Co., 1993.

Loverro, Thom. *Washington Redskins*. Dallas: Taylor Publishing Co., 1996.

Madden, John. *Hey, Wait a Minute! I Wrote a Book!* New York: Villard Books, 1984.

Madden, John, with Dave Anderson. *All Madden*. New York: Harper Collins, 1996.

Mendelson, Abby. *The Pittsburgh Steelers*. Dallas: Taylor Publishing Co., 1996.

Rathet, Mike, and Don Smith. *Their Deeds and Dogged Faith*. New York: Rutledge Books, 1984.

Sahadi, Lou. *Super Sundays I—XVI*. Chicago: Contemporary Books, 1980.

Thorn, John, with David Reuther. *The Armchair Quarterback*. New York: Charles Scribner's & Sons, 1982.

Whittingham, Richard. *Bears in Their Own Words*. Chicago: Contemporary Books, 1991.

———. *The Chicago Bears*. Chicago: Rand McNally, 1979.

———. *The Dallas Cowboys*. New York: Harper & Row, 1981.

———. *The Giants*. New York: Harper & Row, 1987.

———. *Giants in Their Own Words*. Chicago: Contemporary Books, 1992.

———. *Sunday Mayhem*. Dallas: Taylor Publishing Co., 1987.

———. *The Washington Redskins*. New York: Simon & Schuster, 1990.

———. *What a Game They Played*. New York: Harper & Row, 1984.

Wiebusch, John. *Lombardi*. Chicago: Triumph Books, 1997.

# INDEX